For Good

For Good

The Church and the Future of Welfare

Samuel Wells, Russell Rook
and David Barclay

CANTERBURY
PRESS
Norwich

© Samuel Wells, Russell Rook and David Barclay 2017

First published in 2017 by the Canterbury Press Norwich
Editorial office
3rd Floor, Invicta House
108–114 Golden Lane
London EC1Y 0TG, UK
www.canterburypress.co.uk

Canterbury Press is an imprint of Hymns Ancient & Modern Ltd
(a registered charity)

Hymns Ancient & Modern® is a registered trademark of Hymns Ancient
& Modern Ltd
13A Hellesdon Park Road, Norwich,
Norfolk NR6 5DR, UK

British Library Cataloguing in Publication data

A catalogue record for this book is available
from the British Library

978 1 78622 023 3

Typeset by Manila Typesetting Company
Printed and bound in Great Britain by
Ashford Colour Press Ltd

Contents

Acknowledgements

This book began in a conversation between Sam Wells, Russ Rook and Steve Holmes. It benefited greatly from conversations and support from Matthew van Duyvenbode and Paul Woolley of the Bible Society and suggestions and challenges from Anna Rowlands, Deputy Director of the Centre for Catholic Studies at Durham University. We are grateful to Sue Garner for research carried out to strengthen the project. Ian Sansbury provided crucial wisdom, experience and collaboration in the later stages.

We hosted two consultations – one near the outset and another near the conclusion of the work – to test our ideas and expose them to scrutiny, enhancement and criticism. We are grateful to those who made valued contributions to the first gathering, including Jessie Joe Jacobs, Steve Chalke, Ruth Dearnley, Jonathan Hellewell, Tom Jackson, Andrew Grinnell and Stephen Holmes. We are likewise indebted to those who offered constructive and critical engagement at the second event, including Nick Spencer, Patrick Shine, Heather Buckingham, Paul Rochester, Joanna King, Stephen Holmes, Gareth Streeter, Ian Geary, Kathy Mohan, John Barclay, Paul Gutteridge, Ellen Loudon, Stuart Keir, Rachel Lampard and Rodie Garland.

Others who have contributed to the thinking behind this project include Luke Bretherton, Maeve Sherlock and Chris Mould. Laura Lord played a key role in researching Chapter 2. Much of the administrative responsibility has been carried by Shermara

Fletcher, Rob Powys-Smith, Helena Tarrant, Tom Poole and Rumbidzai Mugadza. Funding from Porticus and Westhill was vital in enabling the project to be completed. The team at St Martin-in-the-Fields have been and remain a constant inspiration towards a vision of the goods.

The Authors

Samuel Wells is a preacher, pastor, writer, broadcaster and theologian. He has served as a Church of England parish priest for 20 years, half of those in areas of social disadvantage; during this time he helped to found and lead the first development trust in the East of England. He spent seven years in North Carolina, where he was Dean of Duke University Chapel. He is Visiting Professor of Christian Ethics at King's College, London. He has published 28 books, including academic studies and textbooks in Christian ethics, and explorations of social mission, liturgy, preaching and Anglican faith. He has been Vicar of St Martin-in-the-Fields, Trafalgar Square, London, since 2012.

Russell Rook is a Partner at the Good Faith Partnership, where he works with leaders in politics and faith. A lifelong Salvationist, Russell worked for the Salvation Army for 18 years before in 2008 founding Chapel St, a charity working with churches and local government to deliver innovative public services in disadvantaged communities. He has contributed to several publications in ethics and social policy and convened many forums around faith and social action. Russell lives in South West London with his family and belongs to Raynes Park Community Church.

David Barclay is a Partner at the Good Faith Partnership, working with leaders across the worlds of faith, politics, business and charity. He was the President of the Oxford University Student

Union before moving to East London and working at the Centre for Theology and Community. There he led the Centre's work helping churches address issues around money and debt, particularly focusing on payday lending and credit unions. David lives with his family in Bethnal Green and is a member of his local Anglican church.

Summary

The basic assumptions and aspirations of the post-war welfare settlement are the subject of intense political debate perceived by some as no longer working and regarded by many as unsustainably expensive. Meanwhile church social action, measured in volunteer hours and emergence of new charities, is rapidly increasing. In the context of such controversy over the future of welfare, what is the best role for, and form of, the churches' social action?

Identifying the issues, this book:

1 Affirms that voluntary social action, whatever impact it may have in society on individuals or structures, is a point of renewal for the churches because it invariably energizes, engages and educates Christians around the realities of poverty, and in many cases changes their hearts and makes their souls grow.
2 Acknowledges that in many ways, while being good for society, the 1940s Beveridge reforms inhibited the churches' own vision of what role they best played in relation to inequality and disadvantage.
3 Highlights the way the 1942 Beveridge Report addresses the 'evils' of Want, Idleness, Ignorance, Disease and Squalor, but notes that a healthy society rests not just on eradicating evils but just as much on cultivating goods.

4 Recognizes that government has a duty (and in most cases is best placed) to address such deficits, but argues that government is seldom the best vehicle for cultivating assets.

5 Suggests that assets grow not simply or solely by eradicating deficits but often through the character and initiative that surface amid adversity – and thus those facing economic disadvantage often embody assets as much as or more than those in more affluent communities.

6 Maintains that civil society in general and churches in particular are uniquely placed and equipped to cultivate assets, and that working 'for good' – and not simply 'against evil' – is the churches' most appropriate role in addressing poverty and disadvantage.

7 Identifies five broad 'goods' that churches and civil society may seek in the face of poverty, in a desire to encourage local churches to articulate corresponding goods they seek in their own social action.

8 Offers five models for how churches can thus work in relation to government to cultivate assets, recognizing that complementary action is not always achievable or timely.

9 Recommends that the churches thus order and prioritize their voluntary social action so as to enhance their potential to cultivate assets and to see their engagement in eradicating deficits as ancillary to this central aim.

In this spirit this book argues that, despite profound concern about the welfare state and understandable anxiety about perceived decline in church attendance, the current political and social circumstances offer much opportunity for renewal of church social action and thereby of church life as a whole.

Introduction

An emerging phenomenon

Not long ago one of us participated in a live social action survey. The poll comprised a guest speaker, 4,000 conference delegates and one simple question: 'Does your congregation deliver a social action project for your local community?' If the response was yes, audience members were asked to stand. The person with the microphone listed examples: food banks, street pastors, debt advice, youth work, breakfast clubs, elderly care. At the mention of each project more and more people got to their feet. By the time he finished, about two-thirds of the auditorium was standing. A moment of silence ensued, and people began to wonder when they could take their seats. 'If I'd asked that question 20 years ago', the speaker said, 'only a few hundred would have stood.'

What had happened over those 20 years was that congregations around the UK had taken up opportunities in a fertile environment, and in many cases sustained or diversified their programmes in a more challenging environment, such that by 2017 church social action in the face of social disadvantage was widespread; but meanwhile what had not yet emerged was a theology, a narrative and an overall ethos behind that action. That is what this short book seeks to provide.

The years 1997–2017 provided for the welfare state ten years of feast followed by ten years of famine. In 1997 New Labour, buoyed by an electoral landslide and a booming economy, pioneered a programme of wide-ranging welfare reforms powered by significant investment in public services, and proclaimed that things could only get better. Tony Blair won two more elections and oversaw the largest programme of welfare reform since Clement Attlee in the 1940s.

In 2008 the country became caught up in a global economic crisis. The government diverted billions into propping up the financial system; amid emergency loans and quantitative easing, banks were bailed and cash was printed. In the aftermath of the crisis, the incoming Conservative-Liberal Democrat Coalition, led by David Cameron, inherited an enormous national debt. From 2010 the government initiated a new wave of welfare reforms. Where their predecessors started with money to spare, right now the treasury cupboard was bare. The subsequent welfare reforms took place alongside unprecedented cuts in public spending. But they were not simply about saving money: they also emerged out of misgivings about the purpose and effects of welfare, and out of a philosophy of making work pay.

The numbers of congregations engaging in social action rose in the early New Labour years – but did not decline in the era of austerity. After 1997 a culture of commissioning, in which government outsourced services to new and different providers, presented many possibilities to more socially minded churches. Several seized the day, delivering welfare, opening state-funded schools, coordinating community regeneration and making the most of the public resources now at their disposal. Organizations such as Faithworks achieved great success in encouraging and equipping local authorities and local churches to work and improve public services together. For certain local congregations the effects of austerity were damaging. Contracts lapsed, funding was cut, projects closed and members of staff were made redundant as ministers and volunteers struggled to sustain the services they had worked so hard to create.

But the trend towards church social action was not inhibited. Throughout the 2010–15 period more social action projects were initiated, while staff and volunteer time continued to increase. The exact reasons for this continued growth are disputed. There were many factors: leftover momentum from the New Labour years, David Cameron's vision of a Big Society, a growing theological awakening, greater political awareness, alarm at the human cost of the cuts and a determination to build and sustain certain relationships. Amid all these dimensions, congregations continued to take up the challenge.

In this book we seek to place the emerging phenomenon of church social action in a larger historical context, stretching back to the Beveridge-inspired welfare reforms of the 1940s; we outline how the 1942 Beveridge Report shaped the social and theological imagination of both church and state; we articulate a clear argument of how Beveridge's vision needs to be modified if the churches are to understand their true role in a new vision of social welfare; and we describe how that new vision might be implemented.

What this book is

This book identifies the growing phenomenon of church social action and seeks to give it a social rationale, theological trajectory and political location.

By 'church social action' we mean activities, projects and programmes adopted by local congregations (sometimes as part of national initiatives) to address particular local disadvantage or advance specific local potential, often in partnership with other agencies and in some cases with local authority or significant charitable funding. The phrase is designed to indicate this isn't simply individual Christians pursuing valuable vocations in places of need – by being, for example, teachers in schools or nurses in hospitals. These are vital and important forms of mission but are not the subject of this study, which focuses on corporate initiatives by local congregations addressing some issue of economic disadvantage and real or perceived poverty.

The idea for the book came out of a recognition of the following things: the Beveridge Report was published on 16 November 1942; it was so comprehensive that the churches had to a significant degree narrowed their social vision to dovetail with it; huge social changes since 1942 had changed much of the soil out of which Beveridge's vision had grown; since the 1990s, churches have developed an increasing number of social action projects with varying kinds of relationship to statutory authorities; yet both the overall ethos and the theological underpinning of these social projects remains underdeveloped. What seemed helpful was for a small group of people grounded in this field to write a short book that told a story, articulated a vision and addressed the issues of this changing landscape. This is that book.

Hence Chapter 1 sets out a vision for church social action. It notes how things have changed since Beveridge, but also identifies the way in which Beveridge's diagnosis and prescription were insufficient to address all the work in society that churches are called to do. It delineates what the state must do from what the churches are better placed to do by distinguishing between addressing deficits and cultivating assets – or goods. The book then seeks to promote the ways church social action advances such goods.

Chapter 2 offers a narrative of how congregations have begun to enter the field of social action projects at a time when the welfare safety net appears to be fraying not just at the edges but in some of what have been perceived as its core areas. At the same time the chapter highlights how unclear and in some cases confused churches have been about what precisely they were seeking to achieve by engagement in provision of services and how liable their efforts have sometimes been to being mis-construed as amateurism or proselytism.

In Chapter 3 we offer and reflect on the results of a survey conducted among participants in a wide range of church social action projects. The focus is largely on the providers rather than the recipients of such initiatives, for the inevitable reasons that recipients (or clients or users) are harder to identify and reach and that such access is invariably mediated by the providers. The survey identifies a broadly fertile ground for the argument set forth in Chapter 1, but with some issues for congregations to address, particularly a tension between those leading projects and the church leaders and congregations out of which those projects emerge.

Chapter 4 presents stories of three congregations that are located in different geographical, ecclesial and denominational settings. These stories amplify, illustrate and enrich the vision, context and experience previously described, offering sufficient detail to explore how projects influence a neighbourhood and reflexively how social action reshapes the life of a congregation.

In Chapter 5 we present a spectrum of kinds of social engage-ment and distinguish five strands that each calibrate the church–state relationship differently. The intention is not to celebrate one and denigrate the others, but to explain how each one, in appropriate circumstances, has significant advantages, and in some cases potential pitfalls, and to help congregations think strategically about which model is most fitting and whether they envisage that model shifting as relationships and context change.

Chapters 6 and 7 provide recommendations and a chart for evaluating how a congregation is progressing towards the goals it has set out, using the five goods identified in Chapter 1 as a template.

What this book is not

This is not a comprehensive survey of church social action, either of its extent or of the attitudes and experiences of leaders, participants, users/clients or voluntary/statutory partners. It has involved some on-the-ground research, but that research plays a largely illustrative rather than determinative role in the argument and the study as a whole. Its reach includes England and to some extent Wales but it does not significantly include Scotland or Northern Ireland. It has paid close attention to developments across the diversity of Church of England, denominational Free Church and nondemoninational Protestant congregations, but has not had extensive interaction with Roman Catholic or Orthodox congregations. These gaps are not intentional but a result of circumstance, in some cases mischance, and the necessity of keeping the scope of the study manageable.

We make no attempt to survey the history of church social action in the years 1947–97. There is no aspiration to cover the full range of Christian engagement in society through wider parachurch charitable initiatives or individual vocations to secular jobs or professions. There is no consideration of the way senior church leaders have the opportunity to influence public policy through consultation processes or membership of the House of Lords. There is no detailed dialogue with a range of literature that has emerged concerning the plight of the welfare state and the churches' role in advocating for the state's duty of care. All of these things are highly relevant but outside the scope of a brief study.

Instead the book is rooted in the several decades' combined ministry and mission experience of its authors across Church of England and Free Church initiatives, largely in local churches and their congregations; in their commitment to keep a strong theological dimension amid the urgency and passion of social action projects; in the theological trajectory of Samuel Wells, *A Nazareth Manifesto: Being with God* (Oxford: Wiley-Blackwell 2015) and its argument that social engagement should be fundamentally 'with', rather than always 'for'; and in the authors' network of partners, colleagues, collaborators and friends, who have provided examples and wisdom and challenge and guidance.

In the 2016 Ken Loach film *I, Daniel Blake* contrasts the protagonist's repeated humiliations in the benefits office and increasing social isolation with the tender relationship he builds up with a family who are also facing hardship and distress. In a paradox with which some have strongly identified, while others have maintained is overdrawn, the state seems only to perceive Daniel's deficits, while his considerable and heart-warming assets are visible to a tragically small circle. The film is a lament that these indisputable goods are incapable of withstanding the withering effects of state diminishment. This book is written to guide churches and congregations in their response to the passions such a story evokes, and to foster renewal not just of social welfare, nor even just of church–state partnerships, but of the churches themselves in their discovery and celebration of the Kingdom of God.

I

A Vision for Church Social Action

Introduction

Seventy years ago a revolution took place in the United Kingdom. The state became the church. The state didn't take over worship, preaching, prayer and Bible study; but it did assume responsibility for a lot of what the church used to do:

- educating the young
- caring for the sick
- supporting those in distress.

The churches thought this was a wonderful thing. These vital parts of the nation's life were now in the hands of those who could pay for them sufficiently, distribute them universally and run them efficiently; and the church could get back to what it was primarily called to do. Which was what, exactly? Deprived of the outward-facing and compassionate ingredients that consistently renewed their life and diversified their make-up, the churches gradually found their purpose and membership narrowing to an increasingly introverted and self-serving agenda. By concentrating on personal faith and spirituality, the churches denied themselves the lifeblood that social engagement had long given them.

Thus the revolution, as the last 70 years have demonstrated, was not altogether great for the church. Meanwhile the new state/ church filled a vast place in the popular imagination, responsible not just for order and security but for well-being and flourishing. If it is becoming apparent that the revolution was not entirely good for the church, it is ever clearer that the revolution wasn't entirely good for the state either. Right now the state is having second thoughts and isn't at all sure it wants to be the church any more. This creates a challenge, but also an opportunity for the churches. Seventy-five years after the Beveridge Report it's time to wonder what a readjustment of the post-war settlement might look like.

Falling out of love

The idea that people in need should be the responsibility not just of their wider families, not simply of their local neighbourhoods, not only of churches and those who make their compassion publicly known, but of the state, is a relatively recent one. The problems people identify in the welfare state today rehearse all the reasons why its adoption was so long delayed: it's expensive, it's impersonal and, to the extent that it discourages thrift and diligence and encourages dishonesty and indolence, it's counterproductive.

It took one great push and a captivating idea to create the welfare state. In the aftermath of the hungry 1930s, and amid the sacrifices of war, William Beveridge identified what he called the five great evils that a reform of social insurance would seek to eradicate. They were Want, Idleness, Ignorance, Disease and Squalor. What Beveridge was aiming for was what he called 'co-operation between the State and the individual'.

From the outset the Church of England fell in love with the welfare state. Archbishop William Temple said of his friend William Beveridge's report that it was 'the first time anyone had set out to embody the whole spirit of the Christian ethic in an Act of Parliament'. The welfare state was extraordinarily popular at its foundation, and has remained so for most of its life. When, at the opening ceremony for the London 2012 Olympics, the National Health Service was portrayed as the climax of British history, it came as a surprise but nonetheless struck a chord. It highlighted the quasi-religious place the NHS holds in the imagination of much of the population. And it indicated how crucial a role the welfare state has played in Britain's sense of itself as a place where no one falls utterly through the safety net, and how, for the most part, Beveridge's most basic aims have indeed been met.

Beveridge would without question be gratified to see the following:

- While economic inequality is much greater than it was 70 years ago, 1940s-scale *want* is rare.
- Likewise, while unemployment is significant and low-paid, unrewarding jobs are widespread, the swathes of *idleness* that Beveridge witnessed in the Great Depression have not been repeated.
- Again, in relation to *ignorance*, there is a real issue of the number of young people not in education, employment or training, and inequality skews opportunity for far too many; but the levels of educational attainment are way beyond the imagination of Rab Butler, whose 1944 Education Act coincided with the Beveridge reforms.
- As to *disease*, the National Health Service is not generally well equipped to address chronic complaints such as heart disease or depression, the increasing isolation of elderly people lies beyond the scope of medical solutions, and the idea that healthcare would get cheaper as people got healthier now seems an absurd pipedream; yet the health of the nation is

immeasurably stronger and people live significantly longer than they did in the 1940s.

• As regards *squalor*, Britain remains critically short of housing, and homelessness, crime and drug addiction are widespread; but in general the living conditions of the nation are immeasurably more comfortable than those our great-grandparents knew.

Let us be clear: these are huge achievements, ones that could not have been made in any other conceivable way, and certainly ones that could never have been imagined had welfare been treated in the piecemeal, unsystematic way that preceded the 1940s reforms. The people of the United Kingdom are rightly proud of what the welfare state has achieved.

So why has Britain fallen out of love with the welfare state? The reason is that the system of benefits is based on two things we all want to do and assumes one thing we all have to do. The problem is we can't do all three of these things simultaneously, and social changes have made that more glaringly obvious than it was in 1942.

What we all want to do and what we yet have to do

The first thing we all want to do is to target resources to those in most need. When you meet a family that's been made homeless or you have a friend who's debilitated by chronic illness, you think, 'This is exactly what the welfare state is all about.' But there are a number of problems with this. One is that working out and proving who's in most need is a complex and laborious business. While civil servants are trying to establish whether people's needs are genuine, those people can sink without trace. This is the territory of means-testing. Means-testing sounds like it's fair and reasonable and economic, but in practice it becomes a discouragement to working long hours and a disincentive to being honest about your resources. The benefit culture becomes an inverse beauty parade where you hide your assets and steer away from getting on the ladder of work because, at the outset, that work may be underpaid.

Another problem with targeting those most in need is that it exacerbates a culture of dependence. Populist politicians like to talk about balancing the stick with the carrot and tend to distinguish between the deserving and undeserving poor. But that rather misses the point. The point is that if you know a safety net is there to catch you, you're more likely to walk across a tightrope. But walking across a tightrope is actually a dangerous thing to do. By providing a safety net, the state demotivates people from making prudent and far-sighted provision for themselves, and from avoiding situations or life choices that place them, their households and their futures on a tightrope. The paradoxical result is that the larger and stronger the safety net is, the more it's likely to be needed.

And that leads us to the second thing we all want to do, which is incentivize and reward the values the Victorians held dear – honest working, caring and saving. This was Beveridge's central concern. The crucial words in the 1942 report were his insistence that the state 'should not stifle incentive, opportunity, responsibility; in establishing a national minimum, it should leave room and encouragement for voluntary action by each individual to provide more than that minimum for himself and his family'. In Galatians 6 Paul says, 'Bear one another's burdens, and in this way you will fulfil the law of Christ.' This is the first principle of the welfare state. But just three verses later, Paul says, 'All must carry their own loads.' This is the second principle. The trouble is it somewhat contradicts the first principle, in theory and in practice.

The key to this second area is the Victorian word 'thrift'. Life has many rainy days, and the wise thing to do is to save up for them. Saving up for them is such a good thing to do it makes sense for the state to encourage the practice, and quite probably for employers to encourage the practice too, by investing in a scheme that can bail people out when they get in trouble and can continue to benefit them in retirement. This is the logic of contributory insurance. The trouble is that this changes the nature of the state from a hospital that cares for people indiscriminately when they're wounded to a bank that they expect to reward them with interest for what they've put in. It turns a population of citizens inhabiting a covenant into an association of consumers asserting a contract. It's psychologically powerful, and democratically attractive, because it affirms that the welfare state is for everyone – and so it highlights one of the primal values in our nature: fairness. But life isn't fair. The whole starting point of the welfare state is that we want to live in a society where those whose lives go terribly (and especially economically) wrong don't drown by falling through the net. To go through your whole life working hard and paying taxes while your neighbour with chronic problems and terrible luck pays no taxes and receives a tide of benefits may not be fair; but it may still be just, and the likelihood is you'd rather be in your own shoes than theirs.

Despite the anomalies and inconsistencies of these two desires, government policy managed until relatively recently to keep them both more or less in harness and still leave the public proud of the system they embodied. But there's an inbuilt flaw. Advances in clinical medicine mean a huge swathe of the national budget goes on more and more sophisticated kinds of healthcare; and greater public health means people live much longer and spend an enormously increased proportion of their life drawing a pension rather than earning a wage. All of that still roughly holds together until economic stagnation and unemployment reduce the number of people paying taxes and increase the number relying on benefits.

And that brings us to the one thing our welfare system needs to do, and that is to pay for itself. The early abandonment of contributory insurance in favour of means-testing created a situation where benefits were paying out more than they were taking in. The result is that, whereas originally social security payments constituted 10 per cent of the national budget, today they have risen to 30 per cent. Instead of covering this cost by raising taxes, governments have borrowed. Today the deficit is so large that servicing it costs as much as the state spends on education. The conclusion is simple: we can't afford to harness the two anomalous commitments of the welfare state any longer. The sick, the unemployed, the chronically disabled, the low-paid and the elderly are as needy as ever: but meeting those needs is bankrupting the whole nation.

What might the churches think and what should the churches do? It's clearly not enough just to complain every time the government tinkers with the benefits system. It's more appropriate to recognize that in celebrating the welfare state the churches have affirmed our moral need as a nation to care for one another. But they have underwritten an assumption that the majority of that care can be subcontracted to the state. In theory that should make that care more systematic, comprehensive and effective. But in practice it enhances a culture in which our primary connection to each other is economic and in which our bonds with one another are ones of utility, rather than of trust and tenderness. We are entitled strangers rather than grateful comrades.

It's time for a new configuration of business, voluntary sector, claimant, wider society and state engagement with poverty and need. It's not necessarily the church's place to prescribe a plan or budget for welfare reform. Instead it seems more appropriate to revisit William Beveridge's original vision. Beveridge identifies the five evils of Want, Idleness, Ignorance, Disease and Squalor. In doing so he assumes the rest of society is more or less fine, and the resources of the state should be directed to addressing the problems of those who are struggling. There are a number of things one might like to question about that starting assumption.

From deficit to asset

Beveridge starts with deficits rather than assets. In other words, he sees in people what they are not, rather than what they are. He can scarcely avoid a template of what a 'normal' or well-functioning person should be, and subtract from that the evils of Want, Idleness, Ignorance, Disease and Squalor. But from the churches' point of view, people are not primarily recipients of the attentions of others or the state. They are primarily persons in their own right. The secret of life, as the churches understand it, is not to secure or amass desirable comforts or accomplishments. It is to turn disadvantage into opportunity, transform challenges into learning, glean wisdom from hardship, and build character through adversity. 'What doesn't kill you makes you stronger' may be a cliché, but it has become so because it articulates that even the most distressing dimensions of life can be turned into assets that develop virtue and enhance resourcefulness. That cliché also hints at a different view of a fulfilled life: not so much one surrounded by security and contentment, but one of constant challenges, the encountering and sometimes overcoming of which constitute reward and satisfaction. Life is very seldom about arrival: it's almost always about being on the way, and thus about the lessons learned, the friendships formed and the discoveries made while en route.

Beveridge was writing during the Second World War. Everyone longed for the war to be over. But the war showed people what they had in common, how much they needed one another, what skills and gifts from each member of the community turned out to be unexpectedly vital, what it's like to work for a common cause, and how personal setback is transformed when swept into a larger narrative. Peace brought many blessings, but it didn't give those things. And neither did the welfare state.

So half the problem of Beveridge, as the churches might see it, is that he builds on the sand of what isn't there rather than the rock of what is there – the judgement of deficit rather than the appreciation of asset. The other half of the problem is that he sees Want, Idleness, Ignorance, Disease and Squalor as problems to be fixed rather than indications of a deeper social impoverishment. Fixing such problems simply turns up other problems; alongside eradicating evils, what society needs to do is to strengthen its deeper goods. In short, *addressing deficits is not the same as cultivating assets.* The churches can never be happy simply with eradicating deficits as a social aspiration. Want is, without question, a scar on society: but simply providing food, shelter and clothing does not itself produce fulfilment, well-being or flourishing. Idleness is desperately wasteful and deeply humiliating: but poorly paid, monotonous, unreliable work that contributes to little or no social good is far from ideal also. Ignorance is a prison: but education is about much more than knowledge transfer; it's about unleashing the often-hidden potential of each person by inspiring their imagination, enlivening their mind, empowering their skills, drawing on their experience and disciplining their desires. Disease is a curse: but health is much more than (and not restricted to) the absence of sickness: it's about exercising one's full faculties and being a blessing to others. Squalor is a symptom and cause of the other evils: yet its opposite is not simply cleanliness, but pride, dignity, aspiration and hope.

The point is this: eradicating Want, Idleness, Ignorance, Disease and Squalor is a worthy aim for the state, but for the churches it cannot be the goal; it is certainly a plausible route towards the goal – but even should that task be completed, the goal may still prove elusive. For the churches, the goal surely must be flourishing (not abolishing want); fulfilment (not abolishing idleness); inspiration (not abolishing ignorance); being a blessing (not abolishing disease); hope (not abolishing squalor). The way to these aspirations often includes eradicating the corresponding evils, but eradicating the evils by no means guarantees the goods, and sometimes goods can be reached without evils being entirely eradicated – as the experience of the 'war spirit' showed. The churches have no particular expertise in eradicating the evils but they have profound investment in affirming, upholding and cultivating the goods. Their name for the goods is the Kingdom of God.

What attention to the goods shows is that these goods are not uniquely (nor even especially) prevalent in the circles of society largely free from Want, Idleness, Ignorance, Disease and Squalor. As the churches see it, it is the absence of such goods, more than the presence of assorted evils, that constitutes the malaise of society, such as it is. The evils will always, in some degree, be with us. But those evils need not obscure the goods, and goods can grow and be experienced even (sometimes especially) in the midst of those evils. For example, in the wake of a terrorist incident or racial attack, community and faith leaders may be stirred to assemble with one another across conventional divides and find common causes, shared projects and significant values to promote together. Likewise in the midst of a spate of burglaries, residents of a neighbourhood may gather and form friendships, articulate concerns and make plans, thereby deepening their common life and experience of trust. Simply stopping the terrorist attacks or the house break-ins may address an evil, but doesn't of itself advance a good: by contrast the goods of trust and friendship can be advanced even in the face of racially motivated violence or endemic burglaries. The key point is that trust, friendship, inspiration, fulfilment and blessing are often at least as thin on the ground in communities that are relatively free of Want, Idleness, Ignorance, Disease and Squalor as in communities that are beset by them. What the state can often do is to address Want, Idleness, Ignorance, Disease and Squalor; what the churches are often better placed to do is to cultivate flourishing, fulfilment, inspiration, blessing and hope.

A different way to make the same point is to highlight where the real loss lies in the case of Want, Idleness, Ignorance, Disease and Squalor. A human rights approach or a perspective that makes judgements about what constitutes a proper human life tends to focus on the injustice or diminishment in the life of the individual – their deprivation of opportunity or advantage or entitlement. But an asset approach, which more behoves the churches, discerns that the deepest loss is to wider society: when a person is in prison, it is not just the individual's own freedom that is curtailed or the state's resources that are drained; more significantly, society misses out on the benefit their skills, energy, intelligence, comradeship and experience could be bringing to others, perhaps a very wide circle. If society experiences its life as scarcity, it is because of the superabundance of talent that has gone to waste. It is not simply the individual that has failed to find a way to express their abilities; it is society that has failed to find a way to receive what that individual has to give. Thus the evils of Want, Idleness, Ignorance, Disease and Squalor name not just symptoms of poverty, but some of the primary inhibitors that prevent the flourishing of everyone.

Five great goods

Thus the challenge, 75 years on from the Beveridge Report, is not so much to assess whether the evils Beveridge named have been eradicated, but to identify the goods society as a whole may aspire to and outline paths towards realizing them. The role of the churches is

- To hold the state to account in addressing the five great evils, since the state is undoubtedly best placed to address them. The churches should resist being pulled into addressing the evils in the state's place and should be articulate in identifying where the state needs to fulfil its indispensable role. When the churches do carry out this role, it should be a short-term prophetic witness of response to crisis, not a quasi-permanent alternative source of welfare.
- Never to assume addressing the evils is identical with advancing the goods. This was the danger in the churches' loving embrace of the 1940s reforms. They were absolutely right to celebrate the state's greater role in addressing the evils; but that simply created a more fertile soil for cultivating the goods, a role the state is not well placed to perform, and is ideally suited to civil society in general and churches in particular.
- To work actively and tirelessly to model and cultivate the goods. This offers the churches a social role that is appropriately modest – because it doesn't demand that they step in where they have relatively little expertise and where the scale of the challenge is enormous – but is eminently achievable, in that it affirms what churches do best, which is create cross-generational community and cherish people for what they are, not what they are not.

Thus the churches' calling in social engagement is primarily to cultivate common goods. What might we regard as five great goods? The following list is illustrative rather than definitive. Each 'good' is one on which the churches have a particular perspective but which might nonetheless be widely endorsed in an interfaith and secular context.

Perhaps the focal good is *relationship*. We've come to believe justice means equipping everyone to stand on their own two feet as isolated individuals. But what the churches call the Kingdom of God is not like that. It's about communal relations of mutual interdependence. It's about reciprocal patterns in which you read to me in my blindness and I listen to you in your despair. The human predicament is fundamentally not so much about the limitations of our circumstances or the shortage of the world's resources but about our isolation from one another, our estrangement from ourselves and our alienation from our planet. For Christians these are all aspects of our disengagement from God. The welfare state cannot heal the profound wounds in our lives made by the breakdown or absence of companionship, trust, healthy mutual reliance and practices of kindness. Efficient bureaucracy can never supply what only human touch and genuine encounter can offer. This is where the work of the church principally lies.

Relationship is fundamental to almost every human good. Profitable work is important: but rewarding work invariably involves collaboration, partnership, negotiation, compromise, regrouping to overcome setbacks, teamwork, collegiality, common endeavour. Even a successful employee, on their last day at the factory or office, looks back more upon the people with whom they've shared their journey than the products or achievements that constitute the tangible outcomes. Working in itself is invariably an experience of working *with*. The most comfortable life can feel lonely, isolated, depressing and meaningless without colleagues to plan with, family to grow with, neighbours to abide with, friends to relax and reflect with.

Meanwhile relationship is the greatest solace in adversity. A problem shared is a problem halved. A challenge encountered with colleagues or friends is likely to be more rewarding and fulfilling than a period of success experienced alone. 'You were there for me when everyone else turned their back on me': such words identify a profound level of solidarity that goes to the depths of human experience. Likewise when someone is in genuine crisis, for example becoming homeless, the most important requirement is for a person to walk with them in a spirit of support, respect, counsel and accountability until such point as they find the stability and security to address whatever it is that has brought them down. Relationship is the essence of flourishing, but also of redemption.

A second good is *creativity*. In Irenaeus of Lyons' words, 'The glory of God is a human being fully alive.' To be fully alive, each one of us needs to be making, crafting, planning, shaping. The tragedy of unemployment is not just the lack of income or the loss of the camaraderie of the workplace, but most of all the stifling of fertile imagination and the suppression of healthy energy. The human body was created to make things and the human mind to envision things, and a welfare benefit alone cannot provide these most basic constituents of existence.

Once again we see that simply eradicating hardship and aspiring to abolish adversity is not the same as cultivating creativity. Challenging circumstances require and foster creativity as much as they discourage them. Those who emerge from poverty invariably require relationship; but that relationship more often than not encourages and releases their creativity – the imaginative and improvisatory response to circumstance that enables them to capitalize on opportunity and turn unhappiness into something beautiful. Creativity is seldom fostered by comfort and security: quite the opposite. Neither does it flourish in controlled environments where everything turns out as planned. It comes about when conventional options have been exhausted and people find new uses for overlooked items or reincorporate rejected ideas whose best setting is only just emerging. Surviving on a very low income takes creativity: being assured of a regular salary does not. When creativity, the harnessing of the hitherto neglected gifts of a community and the overcoming of adversity all combine, what results is a peak human experience.

A third good is *partnership*. Whereas relationship is interaction for its own sake, partnership is collaboration for a common goal. We could call relationship 'being with' and partnership 'working with'. Relationship – interpersonal trust, enjoyment, support and understanding – is primary, because it has no purpose beyond affirming the most important things in life, such as love, goodness and truth. It is a final good, rather than an instrumental good – an end, rather than a means of getting there. But partnership has a unique ability to surface qualities in the other that they didn't previously know were there. Partnership is where dignity emerges, as each person's contribution is valued, and where diversity is enshrined, since it takes all kinds of people to achieve a larger aim. To be alone is to be isolated, to be in relationship is to be loved, but to be a member of a team is a thrilling experience of becoming more than yourself and of a group discovering it can be greater than the sum of its parts. Central to human experience is the discovery that challenge and setback unlock hidden gifts and create new partnerships. The answer to adversity can never simply be a monetary concession. Life begins when we turn trials into opportunities and when we make adversity a training ground for character.

Partnership involves the humility that one cannot do everything on one's own and the attention that perceives what other persons can uniquely and beneficially bring. When two parties are at enmity, they have simply not yet perceived or found a way to harness what each side can bring to a partnership. Partnership is not about one party having all the wisdom, resources, experience, knowledge, influence and the other party having simply Want, Idleness, Ignorance, Disease and/or Squalor. In partnerships, individuals and groups discover what can be done when you stop trying to do it all yourself or get an advantage over everyone else, and recognize the gifts and contributions of others and the satisfaction that comes from working together.

A fourth good is *compassion*. However fulfilled our life is, it meets its true end when we are in solidarity with those less fortunate. The centre of the Christian faith is God's longing to be in relationship with us, a desire not inhibited by our fragility and fecklessness, and a desire embodied in Christ. Thus, for the churches, encounters with poverty are not the reluctant exercise of grudging duty but the entry point to an interface with the incarnate Jesus and the stepping-off point to the meeting of our own unnamed, unrecognized but nonetheless deep-seated need. Compassion isn't about supposedly affluent churches reaching out to the patronized 'needy'; everyone knows someone facing even greater adversity than themselves; disadvantage is relative, not absolute; it is part of a healthy life for every person to feel and exercise compassion towards others. Coming into relationship with disadvantaged people is something whatever system we have should be looking to facilitate rather than to abolish. Welfare cannot simply be regarded as the management and eradication of need, because need is the single most poignant place of our encounter with God.

Once again the danger in Beveridge's deficit approach is to assume the goal is self-supporting independent individuals. Such a goal may be a fantasy; even if it is not a fantasy, it is not heaven. Such individuals inevitably regard relationship as the exception to self-determination, creativity as an idle hobby, and partnership as an unnecessary diversion. Compassion assumes mutual interdependence: life is made up of moments of advantage and disadvantage, and compassion names the urge to see difference as the opportunity to establish relationship, engage feeling, offer tangible exchange and build partnership. Sometimes one will give, other times one will receive: to do the first requires generosity, to do the second requires humility. Generosity and humility are two of the great goods of human community.

The ultimate good is *joy*. There is no use handwringing and despairing that our nation can no longer afford the blanket of well-intentioned anomalies, compromises and inconsistencies we call the welfare state. We can focus on scarcities all we like, but the secret of happiness and the key to the Kingdom is to enjoy the things that God gives us in plenty. Life is full of structural injustice and inherited unfairness and circumstantial inequality. But while the churches work and walk and campaign with people to address and endure and change such things, they also proclaim a peace that passes understanding, a joy found in Jesus' desiring and a love that never lets us go. Archbishop Temple may have been right that Beveridge sought to embody the spirit of Christianity in an Act of Parliament, but the truth is Christianity can't be legislated, it can only be lived, and if the churches concentrate too much on what the state should do through welfare they can lose sight of what welfare can never do.

Welfare is simply about the conviction that every member of society should have the opportunity to fare well. In this definition it's easy to focus on the words 'every' and 'opportunity', and to lose sight of what it genuinely means to 'fare well'. There will long, perhaps always, be a role for the state in alleviating the deficits of society. But the church is invariably better placed than the state to cultivate society's assets – its social goods that can be apparent in adversity as much as comfort, and as absent in places of splendour as much as of squalor. Reflection on the Beveridge Report 75 years after its publication offers the

17

churches a moment to identify those goods, to examine closely how its activities are uniquely suited to advance them, and to refine its practice so as to make itself better at doing so. In the process, the churches may well enhance society: but they will undoubtedly renew themselves.

The days when the churches could subcontract their conscience to the government may be coming to an end. The days when the churches resume their constant quest to see the face of Christ in the poor and to base their work and worship there may be about to begin again.

2

The Context of Church Social Action

Introduction

The welfare state is struggling, perhaps like never before. For a variety of demographic, economic and political reasons, gaps are appearing in the safety net, and evident social need is on the rise. At the same time the state, at both a national and local level, is opening up to partnerships with outside organizations in an unprecedented way, creating conditions for new actors to take a growing role in the provision of public services and community-building activities. Among these actors are the churches, which, despite a backdrop of numerical decline, seem to have increased their social activity dramatically in recent years. This rise in church social action has not been free from controversy, with anxiety that churches are masking the retreating state, diluting their distinctive message, neglecting their 'core' activities, or using social action as a cover for proselytism. It is in this context, in which Christian social practice seems to have run ahead of theory, that the vision of a goods approach seeks to speak.

The fraying safety net

> Britain cannot possibly afford its welfare state for much longer. (Peter Hitchens, *Daily Mail*, 2013)

Your public services are in crisis. (Unison Trade Union, advert on London Underground, 2017)

In December 2014 the All-Party Parliamentary Inquiry into Hunger in the UK published its report *Feeding Britain*. The report, produced by a group that included more Conservative than Labour representatives, opened with this striking claim:

Something fundamental is happening in advanced Western economies which throws into doubt the effectiveness of a national minimum below which no one is allowed to fall. It is the erosion of an effective national minimum that has led to the existence of hunger and the rise of the food bank movement in its wake.[1]

The rise of extreme hunger in one of the wealthiest countries in the world has been the most shocking symptom of the problems in Britain's welfare settlement. Some of the evidence received by the inquiry about the levels of food poverty in the UK in recent years was stark. Oxfam and Church Action on Poverty estimated in May 2013 that 500,000 people were reliant on emergency food assistance.[2] The Trussell Trust submitted evidence to the inquiry showing how food banks that had been open for three years or more saw an average increase in the numbers of people helped of 51 per cent in 2013–14 over 2012–13. The Trust's figures for 2016–17 show that it provided 1,182,954 three-day emergency food supplies. The conclusion of the inquiry was emphatic: 'The evidence presented to the inquiry overwhelmingly suggests that

---

1 *Feeding Britain*, report of the All-Party Parliamentary Inquiry into Hunger, December 2014.
2 Niall Cooper and Sarah Dumpleton, *Walking the Breadline: The Scandal of Food Poverty in 21st Century Britain*, Oxfam and Church Action on Poverty, May 2013.

demand for emergency food assistance has rapidly increased over the last decade.'[3]

While hunger and the need for emergency food assistance might be the most visible sign of the fraying of the welfare safety net, it is far from the only one. Homelessness and rough sleeping – an issue that was steadily decreasing in the first decade of the twenty-first century – is now again on the rise. According to figures collected in the latter part of 2016, over 4,000 people were estimated to be sleeping outside in the UK on any given night. This is an increase of 13 per cent from the previous year, and a striking 134 per cent rise since 2010.[4] Over 58,000 households were accepted by local authorities as statutory homeless in 2015/16 – a 44 per cent increase since 2009/10.[5] As the chief executive of the homeless charity St Mungo's put it in December 2016, 'The degree of need is much, much higher than it was even three years ago.'[6]

The other totemic sign of the travails of the welfare state is the growing sense of crisis in the NHS. In January 2017, 23 hospitals were forced to declare a 'black alert' after becoming so overcrowded that they could no longer guarantee patient safety or provide the full range of normal services. In the same month, the British Red Cross controversially described overcrowding in British Accident and Emergency wards as a 'humanitarian crisis'. In March 2017, NHS Providers (a trade body representing acute, ambulance, community and mental health services) issued a series of bleak warnings concerning the challenges facing the system. Chief executive Chris Hopson said 'We now have a body of evidence showing that, with resources available, the NHS can no longer deliver what the NHS Constitution

---

3 www.trusselltrust.org/news-and-blog/latest-stats/.
4 www.homeless.org.uk/facts/homelessness-in-numbers/rough-sleeping/rough-sleeping-our-analysis.
5 www.crisis.org.uk/media/236823/homelessness_monitor_england_2017.pdf.
6 www.theguardian.com/society/2016/dec/04/rough-sleeper-numbers-homeless.

requires', concluding that 'we fear that patient safety is increasingly at risk'.[7]

Much more could be written about the scale and nature of
the holes in Britain's welfare system. Few would claim that what
we are currently witnessing is comparable to the 1930s and 40s
levels of disease, squalor, want, ignorance and idleness that pro-
voked Beveridge's report. But what is undeniable is that gaps
are beginning to open up in the state-provided safety net, and
increasing numbers of people are falling through those gaps into
ill-health, hunger, homelessness and destitution.

Rising needs, declining resources

Who is responsible for this fraying of the social safety net? One
answer is that the welfare state is a victim of its own success.
Life expectancy in the UK is now 13 years longer than when the
NHS was first created, and, as people live ever longer, the costs
of providing them with healthcare and pensions rises inexorably.
The share of public spending accounted for by health is now
at a historic high of 29.7 per cent, while spending on pensions
represents more than 40 per cent of the entire welfare budget.[8]
Projections for life expectancy and the costs of social care for the
elderly suggest that this pattern is unlikely to change any time
soon, and the effects of demography on the viability of the welfare state as we know it are set to become more and more acute.

If demographic change has made the social safety net increasingly expensive to maintain, in the last decade changes in the
economy have clearly made that burden harder to bear. In the
heady early years of the twenty-first century, as politicians
boasted that they had ended 'boom and bust', coping with the

7 www.bbc.co.uk/news/health-39316963.
8 www.ifs.org.uk/publications/8879 and http://visual.ons.gov.uk/welfare-spending/.

rising demographic costs of welfare was manageable. Spending on health and benefits rose substantially in real terms throughout the years leading up to the financial crash of 2007–08, as New Labour used the proceeds of economic growth to maintain and even strengthen the welfare safety net. The financial crisis, and the recession that followed, ended the viability of this model; and the global economy shows no signs of being able to generate the levels of growth needed to revive it. Modern capitalism may have picked up the bill for social security for a time, but those days appear to be over, at least for the foreseeable future.

Of course in the end politicians make the decisions to strengthen or weaken state social provision. With costs driven up by demography and revenue hit by economic crisis, the UK government was left with three possible options: increase already historically high levels of borrowing and debt, raise taxes or cut spending. The Coalition government of 2010–15 and its Conservative successor chose the third option – austerity: that has left the different elements of the welfare safety net struggling to do more with less. While Conservative politicians frequently point out that the NHS budget has increased every year since 2010, the King's Fund has shown that we are now living through the largest ever sustained reduction in health spending as a percentage of GDP since Beveridge.[9] Some local authorities have had their budgets cut by almost 50 per cent since 2010, with another 30 per cent of cuts planned to 2020.[10] A survey conducted by the Local Government Information Unit in February 2017 found that over 40 per cent of councils anticipate 'making cuts in frontline services, which will be evident to the public', with this number rising to over 70 per cent for those councils that provide social care. The Social Fund, which provided community – care grants and crisis loans,

9 www.kingsfund.org.uk/blog/2015/10/nhs-spending-squeezed-never.
10 www.londoncouncils.gov.uk/node/28157.

was abolished in 2013, with a smaller sum of money given to local authorities to design their own replacement schemes.

Some would go even further, and accuse the government not just of passively allowing the welfare safety net to fray but actively promoting its reduction, particularly through welfare policy that uses sanctions and deprivation as a tool to incentivize or discourage particular behaviours. The statistics relating to food banks seem to bear this out: a significant proportion of users (42 per cent in 2016–17) were driven there by delays or changes to their benefits.[11] Some might argue that this is a price worth paying to fix a system that trapped people in positions of dependence and to encourage more into work, and would point to steadily declining unemployment figures as a sign of success. But there can be no doubt that any such gains come at a cost; that cost is often witnessed by churches operating on the front line in Britain's most deprived communities.

The enabling state?

Defenders of the government would of course argue that a reduction in the activity of the state is hardly the only story when it comes to welfare and poverty, and that policy in recent years has been marked as much by new opportunities for churches and other non-state actors to engage in the delivery of public and community services as it has by budget cuts.

The language of 'the Big Society' may have faded from political discourse, but the desire to localize, outsource or seek delivery partners for services traditionally restricted to central government remains an ongoing and widely supported feature of policy-making since 2010. The historic Coalition Agreement of 2010

---

11 www.trusselltrust.org/news-and-blog/latest-stats/end-year-stats/.

boldly declared that 'the time has come to disperse power more widely in Britain today'. Minister of State for Decentralization Greg Clark explained in 2011 the government's view:

> For too long, central government has hoarded and concentrated power. Trying to improve people's lives by imposing decisions, setting targets and demanding inspections from Whitehall simply doesn't work. It creates bureaucracy. It leaves no room for adaptation to reflect local circumstances or innovation to deliver services more effectively and at lower cost. And it leaves people feeling 'done to' and imposed upon – the very opposite of the sense of participation and involvement on which a healthy democracy thrives.

The solution, he said, 'is not for central government to try and seize all the power and responsibility for itself. It is to help people and their locally elected representatives to achieve their own ambitions. This is the essence of the Big Society.'[12]

The major legislation that sought to put this rhetoric into action was the Localism Act of 2011. The Act paved the way for a new generation of elected mayors. It also began a process of enshrining new rights, allowing local and community groups to engage in public service delivery. The Community Right to Challenge gave groups the chance to express an interest in taking over the running of a local authority service. The Community Right to Bid made it easier for organizations to take ownership of local assets such as community centres, libraries, swimming pools and pubs. The Community Right to Build created a process by which groups could put forward development proposals without requiring a separate traditional planning application.

---

12 www.gov.uk/government/uploads/system/uploads/attachment_data/file /5959/1896534.pdf.

The other major plank of government policy putting flesh on the bones of its desire to engage non-governmental actors in poverty-related activity has been a significant focus on social investment. In 2011 the government set out a plan to grow the social investment market. It followed this up by investing £400 million from dormant bank accounts into Big Society Capital, billed as 'the world's first social investment bank'. It also established a Centre for Social Impact Bonds, and by 2016 had invested over £70 million in 32 such bonds. This activity enabled the Minister for Civil Society to boast recently that 'the UK is widely recognised as the most advanced social investment market in the world'.[13]

The government has not developed these plans on its own. It has been encouraged in this direction by a growing number of thinkers and organizations developing ideas for how the state can partner with and support others to play a bigger role in the provision of social services. Steve Hilton, an influential adviser at the start of the Coalition government, has long been an advocate for decentralization and government finding creative ways to give away powers to 'more human' institutions.[14] Meanwhile the Centre for Social Justice, set up by Iain Duncan Smith in 2004, has generated a number of reports on issues in this area. For example, their 'Social Solutions' project in 2014 described itself as a 'challenge for government to take action' in order to 'support a vibrant [social] sector, with a greater role in public services, a better reach into the most deprived communities and stronger relationships with other parts of society'.[15]

---

13 www.gov.uk/government/uploads/system/uploads/attachment_data/file /507215/6.1804_SIFT_Strategy_260216_FINAL_web.pdf.
14 Steve Hilton, *More Human,* London: WH Allen, 2015.
15 www.centreforsocialjustice.org.uk/core/wp-content/uploads/2016/08 /CSJJ2458_Social_Sector_Report_A4_08.14_WEB.pdf.

Critics of the recent governments have questioned the effectiveness of some of these policies, pointing out that new investment has usually been dwarfed by the scale of funding cuts to the third sector and arguing for further reforms to open up opportunities for community groups to engage in public service delivery. But despite this, there has been a broad acceptance across the political spectrum that devolution, localism and partnership with third-sector and faith-based organizations are the right goals for central government.

There is anecdotal evidence that this cultural change is indeed happening within central and local government, leading to a new openness to working with churches. A number of the leaders of church social action projects that we interviewed felt that, prior to 2010, local authorities regarded voluntary sector and faith providers as 'amateurish'. But since that time the combination of localism policies and budget cuts have led to a new reliance on church and third-sector provision. One person commented that 'I know of one manager [of a church-based service] who is now invited to lots of meetings when she wasn't before, even though before the service was just as good as it is now.'

Churches are therefore facing the challenges not only of rising social need and a retreating state, but also heightened expectation driven by successive governments committed to involving private, voluntary and faith organizations in welfare and community building.

The rise of church social action

As the welfare safety net has frayed, and the government has looked outside itself for solutions, a quite remarkable thing has happened: the churches have stepped up. While some increase in activity might have been expected from organizations with a professed mission to serve those in destitution and on the margins of society, the scale of change has surely taken even the most upbeat church advocate by surprise.

While comprehensive data on a category of activity as amorphous as church social action is hard to come by, what does exist suggests a notable upsurge. The most significant evidence comes from the biennial national church and social action survey conducted by Jubilee Plus. Its 2014 results showed a total of 114.8 million volunteer hours were being spent on church social action, a rise of 59.4 per cent from 2010.[16] Within the Church of England, surveys by the Church Urban Fund have shown a similar trend towards greater engagement. In 2014, 59 per cent of surveyed clergy agreed strongly with the statement that 'engaging with the poor and marginalised in the local area is a vital activity for a healthy church'; up from 45 per cent in 2011. The Church Urban Fund also found that over 90 per cent of churches by 2014 were addressing at least one social issue in their local area, with the average church addressing seven different issues and one-third tackling nine or more.[17] The Cinnamon Network's Faith Action Audit in 2016 valued the time of church and other faith groups on social action projects at over £3 billion per year, while a ComRes survey commissioned by Theos estimated that 10 million adults in the UK use church-based community services.[18]

The issue that has galvanized church social action is food poverty. The Church Urban Fund surveys found that one-third of Church of England churches were involved in food banks in

---

16 https://jubilee-plus.org/docs/Report-National-Church-Social-Action-Survey-2014-Executive-Summary.pdf.
17 www.cuf.org.uk/church-in-action-2015.
18 www.cinnamonnetwork.co.uk/wp-content/uploads/2016/08/Cinnamon-Faith-Action-Audit-Report-2016.pdf and www.theosthinktank.co.uk/files/files/Doing%20Good%205.pdf.

2011, with that number doubling to two-thirds by 2014. The Trussell Trust now runs a network of 427 food banks, the vast majority of which are based in churches. Between them they gave out 1,182,954 food packages from April 2016 to March 2017, up from just 25,899 in 2008–09.[19]

If the self-reporting of churches and faith-based organizations is one indicator of a rise in church-based social action, another is the new interest in this area from a number of secular think tanks. New Philanthropy Capital was set up in 2002 as a consultancy and think tank to support charities and funders to have the greatest possible social impact. In 2014 it launched its first ever programme looking into faith-based charities, stating:

> With so many charities working in this space, collectively spending hundreds of millions of pounds each year and harnessing the skills of thousands of volunteers and paid staff, it is the right time to start thinking in more detail about faith-based charities.[20]

Its research found that of 188,000 charities registered in the UK, almost 50,000 are faith-based. These charities receive £16 billion per year in income – 23 per cent of the whole sector. It also found that, in the past ten years, the proportion of Christian charities (38 per cent) that had registered with the Charity Commission was significantly higher than that of non-faith-based ones (24 per cent), suggesting a vitality among Christian organizations exceeding that in wider society.[21]

Other organizations have recorded similarly positive views of faith-based social action. In 2013 Demos, the centre-left think

---

19 www.trusselltrust.org/news-and-blog/latest-stats/end-year-stats/#fy-2011-2012.
20 www.thinknpc.org/publications/questions-of-faith/.
21 www.thinknpc.org/publications/what-a-difference-faith-makes/.

tank, produced a series of reports called 'The Faith Collection'. In *Faithful Citizens*, they concluded that 'Our research suggests that religious citizens in the UK are more likely to be civically engaged and politically active than their non-religious counterparts', and that, 'Despite the trend of decreasing religiosity in the UK, religion remains important to a broad range of active and engaged citizens – and so it must to politicians.' In *Faithful Providers* Demos looked at the role of faith-based organizations in public service delivery, a topic on which many on the left of politics in the UK are traditionally squeamish. Demos, however, concluded:

> 'We found little evidence to confirm critics' fears about faith group service providers: that their main motivation is proselytising, they are exclusivist and they discriminate. Rather, faithful providers are highly motivated and effective, and often serve as the permanent and persistent pillars of community action within local communities.[22]

If Demos has provided from the left of politics a positive secular voice on the role of faith, Res Publica has done something similar from the centre-right. Its report *Holistic Mission: Social Action and the Church of England* argued: 'The Church has the potential, the experience and the capacity to become one of the foundational enabling and mediating institutions that the country so desperately needs.' As with Demos' work, Res Publica's research found that 'Levels of social action are considerably higher amongst Church attendees than the general public' and that 'Fears of proselytism appear ill-founded'.[23]

---

22 www.demos.co.uk/files/DEMOS_The_Faith_Collection_-_web_version.pdf? 1379811908.
23 www.respublica.org.uk/wp-content/uploads/2013/07/mfp_ResPublica -Holistic-Mission-FULL-REPORT-10July2013.pdf.

Taken together, this flurry of positive interest in the role of faith, and particularly church-based social action, suggests an increasingly visible presence of such projects, prompting reflection not just from within the Christian community but also from those in wider society. As Demos highlighted, this rising profile for church-based social action is made all the more remarkable by coming at a time when religious attendance and affiliation continues to decline. While many in the churches point out that the picture across the country is not a simple and uniform decline, there is no denying the overall trend. The religion and society think tank Theos reviewed the data thoroughly for its report *Doing Good: A Future for Christianity in the 21st Century*, and concluded:

> The picture is a sobering one (at least for Christians). Although not as precipitous or monolithic as some imagine, the story is one of (much) lower levels of affiliation combined with (slightly) lower levels of attendance, albeit attenuated by changing temporal, geographical and denominational patterns.[24]

A state of confusion: the churches' view of their role in welfare

> The voluntary sector has been unable to step confidently into the space from which government has retreated. (Oasis, *Faith in Public Service*, 2016)

It might be expected that the remarkable rise of church-based social action in the UK would be accompanied by a renewed confidence and clarity about the role and purpose of such

---

24 www.theosthinktank.co.uk/publications/2016/12/14/doing-good-a-future-for-christianity-in-the-21st-century.

activity as part of the churches' mission. Yet the attitude of most Christians about how and why their church should be engaging with the most vulnerable and marginalized in society would be more accurately described as confused and conflicted rather than confident and clear. The uncertainty emerges in two main forms. First there is a concern that the churches' increased activity could mask, or even incentivize, the retreat of the state from its proper moral duties. And second there is a fear that an increased focus on social action could dilute the core identity and fundamental purpose of the church.

Many commentators in recent years have pointed out that, whatever role churches may play in serving the vulnerable and marginalized, they should not obscure the proper role of the state or the impact of recent welfare policy changes. While many Christians from across the political spectrum welcomed the language of the Big Society, many have been highly critical of its impact (or lack thereof). As Malcolm Brown, Director of the Church of England's Mission and Public Affairs Department, put it, 'The Church, at many levels, strongly supported the Big Society principle. Three years on, we have seen very little of the Big Society.' The implication for church social action was clear: 'The contribution of Christians to hundreds of social action projects which alleviate poverty in many ways is considerable . . . but those most involved know that it is not filling the gap left by cuts to welfare provision.'[25]

Indeed Christian leaders and organizations have been at the forefront of those criticizing recent governments for the fraying of the welfare safety net explored above. In 2015 the Joint Public Issues Team (comprising the Baptists, the Church of Scotland, the Methodist Church and the United Reformed Church) produced

25 www.theosthinktank.co.uk/files/files/Reports/The%20future%20of%20 welfare%20a%20theos%20collection%20combined.pdf.

the excoriating report entitled *Enough*. Aimed at the government's Welfare Reform and Work Bill, it argued that the Bill 'will make poor people poorer' and that 'the hardship caused is likely to be substantial'. The report cited the Beveridge Report and the establishment of the welfare state, explaining that 'We are asking that the welfare state holds to its founding principles, and seeks to provide enough for a basic standard of living, so that every family and every child can survive and thrive.'[26] In a similar vein, Church Action on Poverty in 2015 published *Restoring Faith in the Safety Net*, which urged the new government 'to reaffirm the centrality of the safety net principle' and to 'take steps to ensure that the holes we have identified in this report are addressed'.[27]

While the intervention of Christian leaders and organizations on the government's welfare responsibilities was arguably much needed, it has cumulatively, and perhaps unwittingly, had the effect of overemphasizing the role of the state to the detriment of the distinctive ends and responsibilities of churches themselves. The preponderance of recent Christian reports on welfare have little or nothing to say about the role that local churches can or should play in addressing poverty or cultivating social goods. The danger is that, for all their growing social impact, churches become defined more by what they believe about the state's role than what they believe about their own. Those who are passionate about these issues would do well to remember the 2008 report *Moral, But No Compass*, written at a time of significantly greater government investment in welfare and the third sector, and yet which complained of 'immense religious illiteracy' on the part of local government officials, politicians and other policymakers, along with a pervasive attitude that voluntary sector

26 www.jointpublicissues.org.uk/wp-content/uploads/enough-report.pdf.
27 www.church-poverty.org.uk/safetynet/report/safetynetreport.

engagement in welfare should be tolerated only on terms set by the state.[28]

The goods vision outlined in the previous chapter mitigates this risk of overemphasizing the role of the state without undermining the important work many are doing to hold the government to account. If churches can be clear in contrasting the fundamental purpose of the state in addressing deficits with the fundamental role of the churches in promoting assets or goods, they have an invaluable guide in plotting a way through the change and complexity that characterize the current context. This contrast allows Christians to play the role of righteous prophet, pointing out injustice and holding those in power to account for it, but it also allows them to play the role of good Samaritan, getting practically involved themselves in a way that flows from the heart of their unique convictions and capabilities. As we will see in Chapter 5, there are a range of different attitudes or postures towards the state that particular church social action projects can take, and each is valid given the appropriate context. But all require a clear sight of the particular strengths and limitations that both state and church bring to the table on issues of welfare and poverty.

The other danger that a church response to poverty in the contemporary climate needs to avoid lies in creating something detached from the core life and mission of the churches themselves. This is a challenge that Pope Francis has identified as critical, warning in a sermon on his first day as pontiff against the church becoming just a 'compassionate NGO'. As the next chapter shows, many of those involved in church social action feel under-supported and under-appreciated by their congregations and church leaders, who often view their activity as an

---

28 Francis Davis, Elizabeth Paulhus and Andrew Bradstock, *Moral, But No Compass*, Chelmsford: Matthew James Publishing, 2008.

'optional extra', or something just for those with a particular calling and passion for social justice, or even worse as a distraction from the fundamental calling of churches to worship God and make disciples. It is common to hear an emphasis on social action within the church being dismissed as representing a 'social gospel' attitude that doesn't take the distinctive beliefs and practices of the Christian faith seriously.

This is a problem to which many are now starting to respond. As Angus Ritchie, Director of the Centre for Theology and Community (CTC), has said:

> The challenge is to move social action from 'foreign affairs' – the preserve of a few enthusiasts in the church, viewed by the majority at best as worthy but peripheral – 'to home affairs' – understood as something that flows from the very heart of the Church's worship and mission.[29]

CTC has recently begun a series of studies looking at the relationship between social action and church growth as a way of identifying practices that allow churches to engage in their communities in ways that could lead to more people joining and becoming Christians. And Theos has coined the phrase 'social liturgy' as a way of describing 'the practice of public commitment to the other that is explicitly rooted in, and shaped by, love of God; working for and "being with" the other while being deliberately God-conscious or priestly'. And yet, as Theos admits, 'much work needs to be done – theologically, practically and politically – to ground and develop social liturgy'.[30]

Here again the goods vision has much to offer. An understanding of church social action that emphasizes only the meeting of

---

29 Angus Ritchie at CUK seminar on 'Community Organising and Church Growth', 15 May 2017.
30 www.theosthinktank.co.uk/files/files/Doing%20Good%205.pdf.

needs might connect to some parts of the Christian tradition and encourage some members of congregations to put their faith into practice. But a vision that puts positive goods front and centre, locates their source in God's activity among the poorest and most marginalized and challenges Christians to cultivate these goods through their social action could reach out beyond the 'usual suspects' in congregations and spark new ways of thinking that get beyond tired traditional models of 'charity' and 'good works'. As the next chapter shows, this task could hardly be more urgent if churches are going to sustain and develop their extraordinary growth in social activity in the face of rising needs and the fraying state safety net.

3

The Experience of Church Social Action

Introduction

For any vision of the distinctive purpose and goals of church social action to succeed, it must engage with how Christians involved in these activities currently think and talk about what they are doing. It was this conviction that led to our commissioning an independent researcher to conduct in-depth interviews with a wide range of people involved in different kinds of church social action. The aim was better to understand their motivations and objectives, and to establish how they connected their practice to their faith and to the life of their congregations.

What we have learned is that a number of people seem to be working with something like a goods approach to their activities, with a particular emphasis on relationship and the language of 'transformation'. Many seem, at the same time, to be discovering rich pay-offs from social action – both for their own faith and for the engagement of others in their community with the Christian message. Yet there appear to be some critical barriers that are preventing a fuller articulation of a goods vision for this work, as well as a gulf between the more 'spiritual' activities of congregations and their social action endeavours. If churches are to enhance their ability to chart a distinctive and impactful course in their engagement with disadvantaged and marginalized people, as well as clarifying their prophetic and political message to the state, they will need help in bridging this gulf and overcoming these barriers.

Method and aims

Our interviews took place between 22 February and 9 March 2017, during which period we spoke to 22 people engaged in church social action projects. They came from a variety of denominations, and were located across England and Wales. Between them the interviewees fulfilled a variety of different roles within their activities. Their projects engaged with young people, ex-offenders, homeless people, asylum seekers and refugees, parents and toddlers, people with learning and physical disabilities, those suffering from addictions, and many others besides.

The purpose of the interviews was to explore the aims and objectives of those involved in these activities, as well as their personal motivation for engagement. We also asked how the reality of what they do is different from their expectations, and how their activity has shaped or challenged their theology and understanding of God. Finally we explored how their involvement has affected their views of the purpose of church, and how their church has engaged with the activity in which they are involved.

Transformation and relationship – a nascent goods vision?

One recurring word used by interviewees in the course of the discussions was 'transformation'. Volunteers, paid staff and clergy seemed motivated by a vision of social, cultural and spiritual transformation that informed a lot of the work they were doing. 'Transformation' is a concept that could easily fit with the goods approach to church social action articulated earlier, suggesting as it does not only an engagement with deficit, lack and brokenness but also an aspiration towards positive goals. Certainly by setting the target of transformation, churches are marking themselves out as having a different and higher ambition than most statutory services, which tend to see their role through the more modest aims of addressing a particular aspect of inequality or meeting a specific need.

Another major theme that emerged from the interviews was the fundamental importance, within church social initiatives, of relationship. A high number of interviewees viewed the formation and development of relationships as a fundamental aspect of their work. For some people there was a sense that relationships were the key means towards the ends of their activities. Thus one person explained: 'All of our approaches are really about listening to and forming a meaningful relationship with people to find out what their real problems are and then starting from there in terms of building solutions around what the real problem is.'

Others went even further and seemed to be articulating the formation of relationships as a crucial end in itself. When asked to describe their aims and objectives, some interviewees said 'to build community together', 'to encourage and enrich family life in order to build stronger communities' and 'to treat people with respect and value because each one is created in [God's] image'. As one person put it, 'Our activities might come and go as they are needed, but the relationships are the things that are meant to endure. So all of it is a means to forming a relationship with people.'

As the first chapter of this book explored, setting relationship as a goal of church social action requires attentiveness to mutuality and interdependence, rather than simple one-way exchanges. And for a number of interviewees it appears that a considerable amount of thought had gone into shaping their activities with exactly this aim in mind. One person explained:

> In our relationships . . . there will have been an exchange, a human exchange, that inevitably leads to a progression. So if I'm asking 'why' questions of somebody, it's because I'm genuinely wanting to know, but that will be reciprocated in some way in an ideal one-to-one situation.

Another person expressed this as 'we're about doing life with, not doing life to', a phrase that recurred in slightly different forms in several interviews.

Relationship therefore seems to be a good to which a significant proportion of Christians are currently directing and shaping their social activity. And this also appears to be the case with the closely linked good of partnership. As Chapter 1 explained, partnership requires an ability to appreciate and facilitate the contribution of everyone, breaking down the conventional barrier between 'service providers' and 'clients' that shapes so much statutory activity. Again this seems to be something to which a number of interviewees were attentive, with plenty of discussion about how projects enabled and facilitated the contribution of everybody involved. One person said, 'We believe that everyone who comes through the door has something to give and something to receive, and it is our job to facilitate that', while another explained that 'We will work with these families who are in dire straits – we help them and then we give them opportunities to help others.' The language of 'empowerment' surfaced across a number of interviews, and several people told stories of how 'recipients' of their activity often supported each other.

What these examples suggest is that the vision of a goods approach to church social action, articulated earlier, is likely to be intelligible to a significant number of current practitioners, because it is a language that they are already speaking, at least in part. And indeed several interviewees noted the way in which their focus on relationships and on partnership made their activity unique and distinctive compared to state-based provision. This played out in a number of practical ways, with many people, for example, expressing unease about using the language of 'service provision' and 'clients'. One explained that 'We don't want to be seen as just providing a service, we want to be providing a means to relationship', while another expressed this sentiment as 'These are not services in that sense because we are trying to connect with the other person as a human being who is equal and on a level with us'.

Barriers to the goods

While there was undoubtedly much material that was consonant with a goods vision of church social action, our interviews also revealed a number of issues that seem to be inhibiting a fuller adoption of this approach.

The first of these is the sheer scale of need, which seems to be confirming some people in a mindset of addressing deficits rather than cultivating assets. One interviewee neatly captured this issue, explaining, 'The problem is huge, and it's nuanced and it's varied. Sometimes it's about relational things and sometimes it's about cultural and political things, and we're not touching that. We're aiming to meet a need.'

It is perhaps unsurprising that for many congregations who are intimately engaged in the most deprived and marginalized communities, the rising tide of social need has limited their vision to stepping into the gap left by the retreating welfare state – mopping up some of the more acute need that is not being met elsewhere. When focused on the structural challenges facing British society, some despair. One interviewee said, 'We don't have solutions, so we provide help to meet the need.' The challenge for people and churches such as these is to find a way to avoid becoming trapped in this position, and instead, out of the understanding such encounter brings, to articulate a more positive vision of the real goods that churches can cultivate. Meeting needs might be a fine place for churches to start their social action, but it is not a destination by itself and if it becomes one it can only lead to more depression and despair as congregations find that they cannot in fact plug the gaps appearing in the welfare safety net.

The second issue holding churches back from a goods approach to social action is a subtler one. A large number of interviewees spoke of the importance of 'unconditional love' and having 'no ulterior motive' when discussing their reasoning and method in social action. For example, one person described the aim of their work as 'To help people in the community with no ulterior motive but because that is the purpose of the church'. While this is an entirely worthy and deeply Christian impulse, there was evidence from the interviews that these ideas could hold people back from thinking carefully about any goods they might legitimately want to be promoting through their activities.

On the theme of relationships, for example, some people expressed the idea that, while relationships might be formed in the course of their activities, 'that is not the aim' – as if aiming to form relationships would constitute an 'ulterior motive' and therefore sully the 'unconditional' nature of the service. Similarly on partnership there was a sense from those who most strongly expressed a desire to show 'unconditional love' that they should not be expecting any contribution from those using their service.

As one person said, 'We wait on them, they sit down at a table, they don't come to a hatch, we serve them and clear up after them.' This kind of one-way gift or provision may be entirely appropriate in some contexts, but there is a danger that when the language of 'unconditional' service is elevated above all else, what results can be a fairly impersonal and disempowering activity. What churches therefore need to do is find ways to express a sense of openness in their activity (i.e., it not being dependent on people ticking certain boxes), and perhaps also a sense of gratuity (i.e., what some people get may be much more than they put in), while at the same time holding on to a positive vision of the overall goals of the activity that may make certain legitimate requests of everyone involved (e.g. to engage in meaningful relationship or to contribute in some way). Such an approach may not be 'unconditional' in the strictest sense of the word, but it is no less distinctive or Christian for that.

The final challenge for a goods approach to church social action concerns the source of such goods. Perhaps unsurprisingly, there was an implicit view from some interviewees that the benefits of their action were coming from the church and being brought into the community. For example, there was some discussion about 'bringing the Kingdom of God into areas of society' where there is injustice. While this might be consistent with a goods approach in some ways, it betrays a world-view that sees the goods as particular possessions or gifts of the church that are lacking in society (particularly in poorer communities) – a situation that therefore requires Christians to take these goods to those places. But as the first chapter explained, the proper goods of church-based social action are as likely (and in some ways more likely) to be found in 'deprived' communities as they are in more affluent ones. And Christians also need to be open to the idea that goods might be present beyond a particular church in a way and to a degree that they are not present within that church. That's why the word 'cultivate' is so important – Christians and churches do not have exclusive possession of the goods, and they need to learn to see their role less as delivery drivers who take them from one place to another and more as gardeners working in someone else's garden. There is a time for deliberately planting something in a place where it doesn't exist, but there is also a time for appreciating and tending beauty in unexpected places.

One hopeful sign on this issue is the reflections of interviewees on what they had learned through involvement in their project. The answers to this question revealed that many had come, through experience, to appreciate exactly this point: that those who go to serve poor communities usually find themselves humbled by the goodness they encounter there. As one person said, 'I've learned a lot about the resilience and love in the community; and a lot of the stereotypes are rubbish.' Another said, 'I had fallen into the trap of being a white, middle-aged, middle-class guy thinking I'm coming to do some good for people, whereas I've encountered much more of a rich understanding of the nature of the unconditional love of God.' Others talked about how they had learned that 'It can be damaging and disempowering to a community if it is just done in a top-down way'. It seems then that the task for the churches is to embed this learning into the design of social action projects, so that future staff and volunteers can start off with an attitude of expecting to see many of the goods they might hope to cultivate already in the lives of those with whom they plan to work.

The impact of social action on the churches

I can barely remember what I was like before this. It's challenged me in all sorts of different ways. (Interviewee)

One of the most striking features of the reflections of those involved in church social action is the extent to which they credit their activities with spurring their own personal growth. Many interviewees were eager to share aspects of their character that they felt had changed for the better. For example, one person said that prior to their engagement, 'I was arrogant and a bit prideful and didn't really associate with other people's problems'; whereas now 'I found myself being more compassionate towards people . . . I have become more tolerant.' Another said, 'I have learnt not to assume I know the other person's story. When relationships go a bit deeper the story is completely different.' For some this was a significant, though painful, process of learning: one person said, 'I have learned that I haven't got it all worked out. It's really, really hard to go through with this learning. It's much easier if I do things the way I've always done them, which is by and large on behalf of or for people rather than with.' It certainly seems to be strong evidence that engagement in social action helps people to become more compassionate, understanding and self-aware. As one person concluded, 'If we weren't involved in working with them, we would be poorer human beings ourselves.'

As well as these important character developments, there was also plenty of evidence to suggest that social action work helped Christians deepen their faith. As one person said, 'I have learned how important it is to walk in obedience to God. There are the most incredible blessings for people who hear God's voice and obey his call.' Another reflected at length about the way their engagement had challenged what they had thought was an already mature faith:

I moved here with a certain arrogance of being reasonably well educated, having a clear understanding of what the gospel is and the fact that these people needed it and also, I guess, a bit of a saviour mentality. I probably wouldn't have been self-aware enough to realize all that. But now I've learnt it massively. I had a church upbringing. My family taught me Scripture, taught me Bible stories and taught me what they meant and actually I read the Bible with people who have never been taught that before and that's really interesting to see things with fresh eyes, because actually it might not be the interpretation that I've inherited. But it's not less valid and perhaps it's more valid. It has helped me see there isn't just one way to read and understand Scripture.

This evidence suggests a latent potential for a congregation's social activity to function as a key learning tool for those involved as volunteers or staff, helping them to explore their faith in more depth than would otherwise be possible. As one church leader put it, 'it's a massive discipleship vehicle for us'.

As well as this clear pay-off for churches in terms of character and spiritual development for volunteers and staff, there was also evidence from the interviewees that church social action was helping those outside the church to develop a more sympathetic attitude towards Christianity. While interviewees were keen to stress that their activities were open to all and that they didn't force their faith on anyone, it was clear from people's experiences and conversations that many had come to change their minds about the Christian faith and the role of churches. One person said, 'We often have very meaningful conversations with them about spiritual things. They are not arguing about God. It's genuine seeking conversations.' Another concluded, 'Over the last three or four years, I would say we have changed the perception of that age group [18 to 24] towards church – and I would say that with confidence.'

The gap between churches and their social action

With so much evidence of the positive effects on the life and mission of churches through social action, one would expect those closely involved to speak glowingly of the relationship between their church and the project with which they work. However it seems there are a number of tensions that cause friction between churches and social action projects. There was a strong sense from some interviewees, for example, that many in their churches did not understand or appreciate the work they were doing. One person described talking to their church about their project as like 'looking at a sea of blank faces. It was like "this doesn't really affect me. It's not my problem," you know.' Another said they had come to the conclusion that 'People go to church to be entertained, to do things they want to, like a holy club. Whatever they say, they're not interested in reaching out to their communities.' It seems that this problem goes beyond just the ordinary members of congregations, too, with one interviewee claiming that 'the most difficult people throughout this whole process have been the church leaders. They just don't get it.'

A number of the people we spoke to expressed frustration that the churches they were involved in seemed to be only interested in their Sunday services and not in activities that took place apart from these. One said, 'The work is recognized more by the people outside the church than those inside the church because it does challenge their idea of church.' Another complained that 'They judge the success of something by how many people come to faith or are in church on a Sunday morning. So if people aren't coming from your group into the church, then you are not being effective, so it's not of God!'

Some people complained that even when their work did lead to new people coming to a Sunday service, members of the congregation were ill-equipped to engage with them. One said, 'You wouldn't believe some of the things that the older congregation said to those families that had come in – things like, "What are you doing here? This isn't for people like you" and "You can't take communion unless you've done this, that or the other."'

As a result of these challenges it seems that some of those closely involved in social action have become cynical about churches. One person explained their view:

> Sadly I think the church today is very much like the Pharisees and the Sadducees. We have a self-righteous attitude – an attitude where we are not portraying Christ as we ought to. The church seems to be more interested in nice buildings and large numbers of people.

Another argue: 'There's no empowerment, there's no engagement, there's no challenge. There's no sharing about the great things that God is doing, there's nothing to get excited about. It's still all about programmes rather than about people.' (Of course our interviewees only gave us one side of this story, and it's hard to believe that, where these gaps between churches and leaders of their social action projects exist, the fault lies always entirely with the churches. But what is clear is that there is much work to be done to make connections between what churches are doing on a Sunday and the community activity that is taking place throughout the week.)

This is a key reason why a goods vision for church social action is so important and so timely. As long as churches operate within a paradigm of 'meeting needs' or 'solving problems' it is hard to see how it will be possible to overcome this issue of people not perceiving social action as core to their collective life. Simply pointing to the rising tide of social need and exhorting Christians to do something about it is not adequate, particularly when many congregations are understandably concerned about their own long-term viability.

Where a goods vision could help is in providing a language that can be understood and applied across all the activities of churches, whether 'internal' and on a Sunday or 'external' and in the community. Cultivating relationship, creativity, partnership, compassion and joy are all things that churches can do through their worship, their fellowship, their prayer *and* through their food bank, their debt work, their project with the homeless. They are also things that self-evidently come from God and are not simply produced by well-meaning Christians by themselves. Naming this, and giving these goods pride of place throughout the lives of churches, could enable more people involved in social action to communicate effectively to their fellow church members what they are doing, and in turn help those people less involved to understand and appreciate the projects as a legitimate and authentic expression of the church's life and mission.

The goods vision also helps churches avoid the twin dangers of social action as surreptitious proselytism or bland volunteerism. Each of the goods that churches will want to promote through their social action is firmly rooted in Christian Scripture and tradition – they are the authentic themes and hallmarks of the story to which churches bear witness of God's activity in the world. And as a result they can easily form the basis – through experience or through conversation – of people in the community coming to a new understanding of the Christian faith, and maybe even choosing to adopt it for themselves. At the same time, however, the goods can be understood and appreciated without having to sign up to a Christian world-view. What this allows churches to do is to have honest conversations with possible partners, funders and other key stakeholders about their intentions. It also enables churches to take a range of different approaches in terms of how proactive they would like to be in

sharing their faith through their social action, something rec-
ommended by Theos in its report *The Problem of Proselytism*.[1]
For example, some may choose to let the goods speak for themselves, and only speak of their roots within the Christian faith if
explicitly asked. Others might choose to be more intentional in
articulating their understanding of where the goods come from,
and in offering opportunities for those engaging in their social
activity to experience that for themselves (through prayer, or
attending a church service, for example).

In this way a goods vision provides a helpful challenge to worthy community activists and Pharasaical church leaders alike; the
challenge to locate social action within the heart of Christian life
as a response to God's activity both in the church and beyond,
and then to engage in that action without either reducing it to
underhand proselytism or bland volunteerism.

---

1 www.theosthinktank.co.uk/files/files/Problem%20of%20Proselytism%20
web%20version.pdf.

4

Examples of Church Social Action

In a world where good news is no news, church social action doesn't make many headlines. This is disappointing, not least because the rise of church social action offers a striking counter-narrative to familiar tales of division and decline within both the church and wider British society. Week by week Christians from every denomination provide good news in practical and powerful ways.

In this chapter we offer stories from three very different congregations. Travelling from what was originally a Pentecostal church in Lancashire to an Anglo-Catholic congregation in the East End of London, by way of a community hub in Birmingham, we glimpse three inspiring expressions of church social action. At each stop along the way we are interested to ask three key questions. What does social action look like for this congregation in this community? How have these congregations cultivated particular goods and what have the results been for both the community and the church? And how have they engaged with the state as a result of their activities?

Life Church, Lancashire

Historically part of the Pentecostal movement, Jeff Brunton describes Life Church as a contemporary Christian community

and congregation. Over the last decade, the Burnley-based congregation has become a driving force for social action in the
Lancashire. The journey began with a moment of revelation.
'Personally speaking,' Brunton explains, 'it was the realization that
the church exists for the people who don't come on Sunday and
that the gospel is good news for the whole person and the whole
of the community.' The wake-up call was amplified by events in
the community. In 2001 Burnley experienced two days of riots. In
the aftermath, politicians, faith leaders and community members
were forced to reflect on the high levels of deprivation and lack of
community cohesion that had contributed to the disturbances. As
the decade wore on and the effects of the financial crisis took hold,
levels of poverty and isolation rose further still. With more than 25
per cent of local residents in receipt of benefits, and local welfare
services struggling to meet the need, more and more people came
to the door of the church for help and for food.

In 2010, with many local families struggling to get by, Life
Church launched its first food bank. This initial social action
project sought to reduce the deficit for families facing food poverty. From the start, however, congregation member Deborah
Clarke, who had worked with the local authority, was determined
that this should be more than just a war on want. As a result she
sought to identify and invest in under-utilized community assets
and to foster long-term relationships with those in need. The most
obvious assets were the people of Burnley themselves. Clarke
began to recruit and train volunteers, initially from the congregation and then from the wider community. She soon discovered
that local residents were more than willing to give their time and
talent, skills and passion to help their neighbours. By assigning
volunteers to deliver food to people's homes, Clarke sought to
reduce stigma and open the door to stronger relationships between
volunteers and food-bank users. Two things soon became clear.
First, the scale of the problem meant that congregation members

would never be able to eradicate food poverty. And, second, food poverty was itself a symptom of a more serious condition, namely social isolation. In the words of Brunton, 'We soon realized that many felt totally abandoned and left out, lonely and hopeless.' The realization paved the way for the creation of Community Solutions, a larger befriending project, recruiting more volunteers to build more relationships with local people. Since that time Community Solutions has developed many different initiatives, each with the common thread of reducing isolation by facilitating friendship.

Having helped to launch Community Solutions, the Life Church congregation itself became a hub for social action. The congregation worked with other churches to provide street pastors in the town centre, staff and volunteers began to care for victims of domestic abuse at a local women's shelter, a team of full-time youth workers provided extracurricular activities in schools across the town and, in 2014, in partnership with the Chapel St Community Schools Trust, Life Church opened Burnley High School, a state-funded Christian ethos school in a new £12 million facility close to the church site.

Delivering these services has led to a far greater connection with local government. Given the range of projects on offer, Life Church has to foster relationships with politicians and officials in different departments. The situation is made more complicated still by the fact that while much of the town's life is governed by Burnley Borough Council, other elements, such as education and children's services, are overseen by Lancashire County Council. As with any relationship, the nature of the congregation's engagement with government has changed over time. Officials at Lancashire County Council recognized the unique work that Community Solutions was doing to increase volunteering in the community and reduce social isolation. For the officials concerned, this asset-based project represented vital work that they were simply not able to do. As a result, funding became available to develop similar services in a number of nearby towns. To do this it became necessary for Community Solutions to become a stand-alone entity. Some churches may have feared this development and the loss of control it represented but, as Brunton points out, 'It is often better to facilitate than control. If the church seeks to control a project it can often limit its impact and growth.' True to his word, over the next few years Community Solutions developed befriending projects, food banks and a range of other initiatives in Burnley, Pendle, Preston and Hyndburn. The story of Community Solutions illustrates the need for agility and flexibility where a congregation's relationship with local government is concerned. Having originally started out working on its own, Life Church was flexible enough to seize the opportunity of partnership with the state to allow its unique approach to grow in scale and impact.

Having said this, the range of social action projects that Life Church hosts and initiates, combined with the complications of working with two governmental bodies, can at times create tensions for its congregation. While the county council was keen to support and fund the work of Community Solutions, the same could not be said of the borough council when Life Church first proposed a new high school. When a congregation collaborates with government on one particular issue, only to contradict the state and campaign on another, the results can be uncomfortable. Leaders at Life Church have had to remain clear about where the church's priorities lie and which battles the congregation are called to fight. Often there can be a price to pay and consequences to face. Choosing to challenge a local authority in one area can result in the withdrawal of government partnership and support in another. That said, in the same way that attitudes to social action can change in the church, so too do the policies and positions of local authorities. In April 2017, Jeff Brunton, as both the pastor of Life Church and Chair of Governors at Burnley High School, addressed hundreds of families at the opening of the school's new campus. Welcoming both the CEO of Burnley Borough Council and the Deputy Mayor, he invited them officially to open the building. Where previously there had been opposition there is now a spirit of collaboration. One of the crucial factors of this change is the ongoing determination of the Life Church congregation to work with the local authority, even in the most difficult times.

Throughout its many activities, Life Church has kept a clear and consistent focus on the goods to which their social action is leading. Mark Hirst is a member of Life Church, a former director of Community Solutions and now the founder of Spacious Place, a new social action initiative working with the congregation. Mark says, 'When anyone connects with us we want them to experience joy.' Every week Hirst sees joy in the most unusual suspects and surprising places, whether in the lives of former offenders at their weekly Street Soccer Academy or the young people employed as part of the paint shop, a social enterprise that recycles and sells unused paint and provides affordable decorating services for the local community. 'Sometimes the people we work with have forgotten how to laugh. One of the joys of my job is to see them laugh again and get to laugh with them.'

In Life Church we witness a discernible pattern for almost all church social action. Beginning by addressing the most obvious needs in the community, the church's focus on relationships allowed it to discover needs that are hidden and assets that are waiting to be unlocked. With a good deal of creativity and a willingness to partner with the state where appropriate, this has led to a whole variety of projects. The ultimate end is that everyone involved can experience genuine joy together. Along the way, members of Life Church have discovered that community transformation brings new life to the congregation. During the time that Life Church has engaged with its community in these new and creative ways, the worshipping congregation has grown by 50 per cent. As a result the church has built a brand new building to host both its growing congregation and all manner of community activities.

Oasis community hub, Birmingham

The Oasis Trust creates community hubs around the world. Founded by Baptist minister Steve Chalke, Oasis exists to 'build healthy communities where everyone can belong, thrive and achieve their God-given potential'. The charity's activities are almost as diverse as the communities it serves. In England, Oasis sponsors 47 state-funded academy schools. These schools offer a Christian-ethos education for children and a hub of social action for the wider community.

In January 2014, Oasis took on a new primary school in Winson Green, Birmingham. Winson Green is a hyper-diverse community; 59 per cent of local residents have lived in the community for less than one year; 10–15 per cent are asylum seekers with no recourse to public funds. The pupils at Oasis Academy Foundry speak 40 different languages, with 74 per cent receiving free school meals. Only a few days after Oasis's arrival, the community became infamous through a series of fly-on-the-wall documentaries. Channel 4's *Benefits Street* painted residents of Winson Green as work-shy benefit claimants enjoying life at the expense of the welfare state. Oasis's new school formed the backdrop to the title sequence. With the community's self-esteem at an all-time low, Oasis staff gathered local residents in the school hall. Together they began to fight back.

Oasis's work in Winson Green is co-led by head teacher Emma Johnson and Anji Barker, the director of the community hub.

Given that it had previously been in special measures, Oasis's first priority was to turn the school around. Along with her team, Emma Johnson worked tirelessly to raise teaching standards and pupil attainment. Upon their next visit, OFSTED judged the Oasis Foundry Academy to be 'good in all areas with outstanding personal development and student welfare'. While rightly proud, Johnson knew that the job of transforming the lives of families and the wider community had only just begun. As she points out, 'There are things that families need that school simply cannot provide.' This is where the community hub comes in. A social worker by training, Anji Barker works alongside the school staff to support vulnerable children and families. She is joined by a small team of Christians who have moved into the area to support local families and participate in the community hub.

Working with staff, parents, children and volunteers, the community hub hosts a wide range of social action projects. Soho United is a local football club that encourages dads and their sons to spend time together, offers some a chance to be scouted by West Bromwich Albion, and helps many more to enjoy regular exercise. Animal Encounters is a more unusual expression of social action. Having purchased a number of animals, including rabbits, sheep and alpacas, the community hub offers animal therapy. This type of activity has been shown to improve the social and emotional well-being of vulnerable individuals, improving motivation and education. Workers at the community hub take the animals into schools, community groups and even the local prison. Through these and other initiatives the hub provides unique opportunities for staff and volunteers to build meaningful relationships in the community. 'We are not here to do things to people or for people', Barker insists. 'We are here to be with people.' Recently, a group of parents expressed interest in parenting classes. Rather than providing the training themselves, the hub team helped the parents to host, promote and facilitate sessions for one another. As a result, a deficit was transformed into an asset.

This model of an Oasis school and community hub requires a more complex set of connections with the state. The Oasis Foundry Academy, for instance, would not exist were it not for the government's decision to entrust the local primary school to Oasis. Furthermore, by nature of the families they serve, teachers, staff and volunteers relate to many other government agencies and departments. These include social services, housing associations, Job Centre Plus, Citizens Advice Bureau, the National Health Service and more besides. Here, the hub provides an essential portal, enabling community members to access vital services and support. The community hub is testimony to the possibilities that collaboration with government can bring. The model clearly heightens the level of political complexity. However, it also provides a unique opportunity to educate and transform the lives of children, while offering a dynamic hub of social action for their families and community.

Oasis's work in the community is not limited to collaboration. The hub team has the opportunity to offer services that complement existing state provision. The hub's Grow Groups provide a useful example of a complementary service. Using a community-based approach, these support groups help members of the community recovering from addiction or suffering poor mental health. The purpose of these groups is to supplement rather than replace the clinical support of doctors and healthcare professionals. As Barker explains, 'Grow Groups complement and offer something different from a professionalized service. People whose lives are very messy find that our approach is often more inclusive and easier to access.'

Much good has come of the Winson Green community hub. Among comparable communities, the Oasis Academy Foundry ranks among the highest-performing schools in the country. Following the nightmare on *Benefits Street*, the combination of a good school and creative community hub is slowly improving the esteem of Winson Green. As Johnson points out, 'Where once families couldn't wait to get away, now they fight to stay.' The relationships formed in the school and the hub are having a transforming effect. This is captured in the story of a mother who, after years of social exclusion, assisted a younger and more bewildered mum to successfully complete her benefit claim. 'As one mother dashed across the playground to hug and embrace the other,' Barker continues, 'all I could see was compassion and joy.' Or the time when a lone parent was told by the Job Centre to apply for cleaning jobs. This task was daunting enough for a mother with four children. However, in her home country she had only ever cleaned with a broom and had no idea how to use modern cleaning products. The hub team recruited her as a volunteer to help clean their community centre and appointed a community member who herself had recently lost her job as a cleaner to be her tutor and trainer. In their moment of mutual need two women found a way to help one another and both found work as a result. In another example of asset-based social action at the community hub, staff organize cookery workshops where Somali mums, who have often felt unwelcome and whose talents have invariably gone unrecognized, teach people from more prosperous neighbourhoods how to make authentic Somalian cuisine.

Unlike Life Church, the Oasis community hub features a newer and less developed form of Christian community. But, just like Life Church, they are finding that spiritual growth and impact in the community go hand in hand. The Christians who moved into Winson Green did so because they felt called to be part of a missional and incarnational community. Alongside the relationships they build with local residents, these volunteers meet to worship and pray in one another's homes and attend services together at a large Anglican church in Birmingham's city centre. As yet, there is no formal expression of church within the community. However, plans are afoot to open a congregation in a local church hall. Barker is confident that this will happen soon.

> We have everything a church has – community meals, youth groups, kids clubs, discipleship, training, support groups, discipleship – except the public worship. We want the church to be owned by local people. Once we have some local people on the discipleship journey we will be ready to launch.

Beginning with a Christian charity, school and missional community, the Winson Green community hub will soon give birth to a new congregation.

St George-in-the-East, London

The final stop on this social action tour is St George-in-the-East, an Anglican congregation in Shadwell, East London. While the church dates back to the eighteenth century, the most recent chapter began in 2015. At this point St George-in-the-East was home to a small and declining congregation comprising 15 regulars, worshipping in a large Grade I listed building surrounded by a deprived and disconnected community. In a bid to make the most of under-utilized space, the church rented out part of the crypt to an organization called the Centre for Theology and Community.

The Centre for Theology and Community (CTC) helps local congregations to engage with their communities, primarily through the methods of broad-based community organizing. Community organizing is the term given to a series of practices that enable diverse groups to effect change through collective action. The founder and director of CTC, Angus Ritchie, considered it hypocritical to help other churches while ignoring the one upstairs. After lengthy discussion, and with the full support of the congregation, Angus Ritchie and Tim Clapton, a colleague at CTC, were appointed as part-time clergy at St. George-in-the-East, with the Rectory housing a lay community. Commencing with a listening campaign, the first stage of any community organizing strategy, the team used their skills to facilitate a new vision for the congregation. From now on the church would prioritize three activities: worshipping God, welcoming neighbours and challenging injustice. The ultimate aim was to renew the worshipping congregation and reconnect the church with its community.

With such a small congregation, the immediate challenge was one of capacity. The church's response was to think creatively and generously about how it could use its assets in partnership with others in the community who shared the same concerns and vision. For example, many in the area were outraged when a Jack the Ripper Museum opened after submitting a highly misleading planning application promising to highlight the role of women in the history of the East End. As well as complaining to the council, St George's decided to take upon itself the task of becoming the site for the true celebration of East London's women. Utilizing the skills and passion of many non-churchgoers in the community, an exhibition called 'East End Women – the Real Story', hosted in the church building, was born.

With this successful experience of social action under their belts, St George's turned its attentions to an ever bigger problem. In 2016 the church hosted the inaugural Shadwell Assembly. An important element of any community organizing strategy, an assembly convenes diverse groups and encourages collective action in response to issues of mutual interest. The Shadwell

Assembly highlighted the lack of affordable housing as one of the most challenging issues for local residents. With the boom in London property prices it has become ever more difficult for those on low wages to afford to live in their own communities. As rents continue to rise, residents must allocate an increasing share of their income to rent, work multiple jobs just to cover the bills, or face the prospect of moving away completely. From here on, St George-in-the-East would become the focal point in the community's campaign to secure a community land trust that could facilitate the creation of new and affordable homes within the community.

The campaign for affordable housing in Shadwell began not with a march but a walk. Before going further, residents had to identify a piece of land that could be used for affordable housing. The community came together to walk their land and spy out potential sites. Even the organizers were doubtful that such a space existed. Much to their surprise, they stumbled across a significant piece of undeveloped land. As Ritchie himself says, 'None of us thought that we'd find anything, but it turns out the land we were looking for was under our nose all along.' Upon further enquiry they discovered that the land belongs to Transport for London. At the 2017 Shadwell Assembly, the community secured the support of the Mayor of Tower Hamlets for their campaign. They are now calling on the Mayor of London and executives of Transport for London to put the land into the hands of a community land trust that will use it for affordable housing. Just like the Jack the Ripper Museum, the housing campaign combines a call to government to act with a recognition that the community itself needs to take responsibility for creating the kind of area that residents want to see.

With so much partnership, facilitation and hosting, it might be feared that St George's social action would be a somewhat diluted affair, with little that was distinctively Christian. But Ritchie is adamant that this is not the case. 'We can convene and we can be hospitable', Ritchie says, 'but we can't be neutral. We are always Christian, always Church.' Through the congregation's efforts and initiatives, there remains a constant commitment to the good news of the gospel and the wider Christian tradition. Meanwhile, since 2014, the worshipping congregation has more than tripled in size. This is worth raising on two counts. First, this is a sign of significant success. After all, the worshipping community is the place where goods often abound. Here men and women find new relationships, means of expression, opportunities to serve, individuals to love and reasons to celebrate. At St George-in-the-East growing numbers of people are participating in the good news of the gospel. Second, certain church leaders worry that greater investment in social action may produce diminishing returns for their worshipping congregation. It is as though a choice has to be made between exciting mission and a thriving congregation. With St George-in-the-East, Ritchie asserts, no such choice had to be made. It's really not a case of either/or but simply both/and. There is a risk, Ritchie points out, that Christian social action is understood as better-off people being charitable to poorer neighbours, whom they assume will never be interested in being part of the church. On the contrary, the congregation of St George-in-the-East has discovered that social action can both enrich the lives of those in congregations while helping those in communities to find their place within congregational life.

Conclusion

These three stories show how churches of different sizes and traditions, in significantly different contexts, can all pursue forms of social action that align with the vision of cultivating goods rather than simply addressing deficits. But even as they do so, they reveal certain core attributes common to churches that want to pursue this approach. First, they share a deep belief that their communities are not primarily places of deficit and problems but of resources and assets waiting to be unlocked. Where others saw only deprivation and injustice, these churches saw skill, talent and compassion waiting to be cultivated. In each case this has led not to worthy problem-solving, which can never meet the scale of need, but rather to open-hearted and joyful creativity which recognizes challenge and deprivation but is not overwhelmed by it. Second, in pursuing these goods all three churches demonstrated a deeply relational approach to social action. When meaningful relationships with a wide range of people in the community are pursued, churches are inevitably drawn into creative forms of activity in order both to solve problems and to create opportunities for joy and flourishing. And, third, all of these churches demonstrated confidence in their core identity and an openness to letting their social action enrich and enlarge the life of their congregation. As a result, they all found that their activities led not only to remarkable social change but also to impressive growth in the congregation size, demonstrating that a vision for social action based on the promotion of goods can break down the artificial barriers between the 'internal' and 'external' aspects of church life.

The other common theme within these stories was a complex and often shifting set of relationships with different state bodies. This seems to be an inevitable feature of churches engaging meaningfully on welfare and poverty-related issues. The next chapter unpicks these tangled threads and looks at the pros and cons of different types of church–state relationships for those with a vision and determination to pursue the goods.

5

Models of Church Social Action

Some say that if two theologians agree on a doctrine, it must be because one of them has had a temporary absence of mind. There is no way that 10,000 congregations in the UK are ever going to adopt exactly the same model of social action. Given the variety of church traditions and of contexts that congregations serve, diversity is inevitable. Yet we argue that church social action should as much as possible be guided by a common vision of cultivating assets and promoting goods within communities. So how can churches that want to live out this vision navigate their way among the huge variety of different projects with which they might want to engage?

In Chapter 1 we argued that a clear-headed look at the welfare state can help churches think through their unique contribution to tackling poverty. In the same vein, exploring the ways different types of church social action relate to the state in its many forms is a useful way of clarifying exactly what a goods vision made flesh might involve in a variety of contexts. We've seen how ongoing reforms in public services and the subsequent debate as to the future of the welfare state has contributed to the rise of church social action. The direction of travel for our public services is indisputably towards a world where government commissions more and delivers less. The state will continue to make all kinds of requests of (and offers to) churches to engage in welfare and community provision. In this context church leaders need to be clear about what social action entails for their congregations. In this chapter we explore a range of modes of social action currently undertaken by local congregations. These demonstrate how churches are delivering the goods in their own communities and engaging with the state as they do so.

A Social Action Spectrum

To explore different models of church social action we have developed a Social Action Spectrum. This spectrum offers a guide by which congregations can reflect upon different modes of social action and respective implications for their interaction with the state.

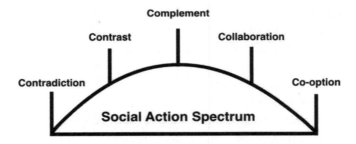

This Social Action Spectrum perceives a graduated approach to church social action. The points along the spectrum capture five distinct modes: Contradiction, Contrast, Complement, Collaboration and Co-option.

Three disclaimers are necessary. First, all of these categories can, in the right circumstances, represent valid expressions of church social action. Some undoubtedly present more opportunities for churches to promote goods in their communities, but it is not a simple case of some of these models being always right and others being always wrong. Each may have its place in the right context and with the right caveats. Second, we are not suggesting that the positions that churches take are fixed. No matter where we live, times change, and eventually so too do churches and governments. Furthermore, church social action is hope-fuelled. In faith we believe that our world can change. As change happens, deficits reduce and people flourish, we should expect congregations to alter their approach and take action in new ways. Likewise, when new problems surface, groups find themselves forgotten or neighbourhoods recognize they are far from the good life, the local church should be ready and waiting to respond. Third, the complexities of community, and the fact that congregations serve different groups at the same time, mean that it is often necessary for churches to take a variety of approaches and foster different forms of social action at the same time. We are not suggesting that churches need to pick one model and stick with it for all their activity. Readers may well plot their own congregation at several points along the spectrum. What is important is that each project or activity understands within which model it fits – and therefore which opportunities or risks might present themselves in pursuing a goods vision.

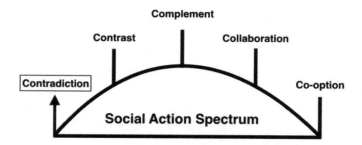

On one end of our spectrum is contradiction. Here churches stand against decisions, policies and sometimes leaders in government that they consider to be corrupt, oppressive or unjust. In this mode, congregations become focused on particular social issues, often speaking up for or with those whose voices are frequently ignored or suppressed in public debate. In the mode of contradiction, social action turns complaints into campaigns. It combines prayer, petition and protest. The ultimate aim is to effect change, right wrongs and overturn injustice. In the mood of contradiction, church social action can remind government of the obligations owed to its most vulnerable citizens.

A recent example of successful contradiction involving churches is the campaign to persuade the government to cap the cost of payday loans. After the financial crisis of 2007–08 the UK saw a spectacular rise in the number of companies providing short-term, unsecured personal loans at interest rates that sometimes topped 10,000 per cent APR. As organizations deeply embedded in communities across the country, churches were among the first to realize the misery that these companies were causing as people desperate for a way to make ends meet or respond to a financial crisis became trapped in spirals of debt. Archbishop of Canterbury Justin Welby gave voice to this growing unrest, labelling payday lenders as 'usurers' and joining with other bishops in the House of Lords in calling for the government to curb the worst excesses of the high-cost credit industry. Along with this high-level lobbying, local churches engaged in grass-roots protest, notably through the Citizens UK Just Money campaign. They called for the government to take responsibility for a situation in which people's lives were becoming blighted by the deficit of debt, and to address this through a cap on the cost of credit as well as the amount of debt anybody could get into through taking out a payday loan. Their efforts proved successful. With defeat in the House of Lords on this issue imminent, the government relented and instructed the Financial Conduct Authority to institute a cap, which came into force at the beginning of 2015. Since that time, the number of complaints about payday lending has fallen by almost half. This example shows how contradicting the government can be a successful way for churches to hold the state to account in fulfilling its basic obligations to help its citizens avoid unnecessary deficits in their lives, such as usurious debt.

The danger with the contradiction model is that it can become addictive. Righteous indignation is an attractive emotion for many people, and protesting against the government can be both morally satisfying and a powerful collective experience. Everybody likes being on the side of Good against Evil. The problem with this is that churches can become stuck in contradiction mode, and begin to view any other models as 'selling out' or settling for less than the ideal. A lazy mindset can develop that sees all problems in society as the responsibility of 'someone else', usually the state. As we have already seen, this position asks too much of government and too little of the churches. Contradiction that asks the state both to address deficit and to promote assets on its own needs to be avoided, and Christians should think seriously about whether what they want to happen can best be achieved by the state acting on its own or with some positive input from churches or others. The reason why Justin Welby's intervention on payday lending was received so well was partly because he didn't just look to the government to do everything, but instead pledged that the Church of England would dedicate its resources towards cultivating assets in building up more responsible forms of lending, such as credit unions.

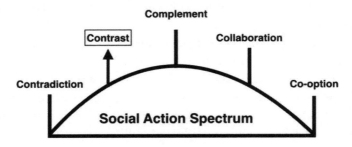

Less confrontational than contradiction is contrast. In this mode congregations seek to offer something very different from government. Usually this will come about where the state operates in an unhelpfully deficit-focused way, and the churches want to bring in an approach that is much more focused on the cultivation of goods.

Homelessness is a prime example. Fundamentally, the state sees homelessness as a deficit problem – people lack shelter, and accordingly it is the government's responsibility to provide them with access to that shelter. The problem is partly that lack of shelter can, in some cases, be simply the tip of an iceberg, hiding beneath the surface a host of complex issues in a person's narrative and circumstances. But even at face value the problem is that the state has limited resources with which to provide shelter, and thus that access is proscribed in a number of different ways. Until recently, local authorities operated with a system of 'priority need', in which they were only obliged to provide help to people who presented as homeless and also fitted into certain additional categories of particular need (such as those with children). Even now the provision offered to people will have a number of conditions attached related to place, either forcing people to stay in their one area of 'local connection' or forcing them to relocate a long way away from their current location. And even for those who do end up with a state-aided roof over their heads, there is often little or no help from the government to deal with the underlying reason why they became homeless in the first place.

Churches are able to see homelessness very differently. They recognize the very real deficits that come with lacking a place to call home, and are willing to meet those through projects like winter night shelters and soup kitchens. But they also see homeless people as people rather than statistics or assemblages of deficits, and are able and willing to put in the time and effort to cultivate the good in them as a way of helping them along the journey to rebuilding their lives. That's why church homeless provision is often deeply relational and is able to engage with people who have entirely dropped out of the state system.

The benefit of this kind of 'contrasting' model of church social action is that it can very clearly distinguish between deficit-focused activity and goods-cultivating activity. Contrasting church social action projects can stand up and stand out, bringing the unique assets of a Christian world-view to bear in a way that generates transformative results for all involved. Where state provision is simply not getting the job done or is treating people as less than they truly are, this can be a critical form of witness. The danger of a contrast mindset comes in circumstances where distinguishing between state-run deficit activity and church-run goods activity is not quite so vital. As we will see, there are other models that can creatively blend the role and resources of church and state in a way that can often achieve a level of scale that churches operating on their own are unlikely ever to manage.

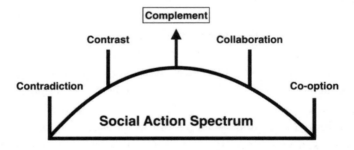

In the middle of the spectrum is complement. Here congregations seek to stand alongside the state welfare system. Where contrast approaches are usually separate from existing state provision, complementary social action is more closely connected. In this mode churches use their own resources to provide dimensions of care and support additional to those made available by the state. Volunteers offer relationships and mentoring, church facilities are used for drop-ins and workshops, staff members receive referrals from government agencies and provide individuals and families with extra care. While occasionally eligible for state funding, these initiatives are often maintained by individual grants and donations and subsidies from local churches.

A great example of this is the work of SPEAR, a programme run through partnerships with local churches. For young people struggling to find work, the state provides the deficit-based intervention of benefit payments (now with the controversial addition of sanctions for those who don't jump through the requisite hoops to prove they are looking for work). To collect these payments, most young people are required to regularly visit Job Centres. But while there, they might find themselves engaged by a SPEAR Centre staff member, who will invite them on to a free six-week course of training and mentoring. During this course the young person will be challenged to let go of a 'victim mentality' and instead adopt a 'power mentality'. (One could call this an explicit move from deficits to assets.) SPEAR coaches will adopt an intensely personalized approach to uncover the young person's skills and ambitions, and at the end of the course the young person will graduate in a public ceremony where they will talk about their experiences and be celebrated for all they have achieved. They will then receive the help and support of a specialist 'careers coach' for up to a year. This approach, which is saturated in an understanding of the goods already present in the lives of young people often dismissed by the rest of society, is spectacularly successful. Over 75 per cent of those who finish the course not only go on to find work or achieve a place on a training or education course, but they are still there a year later. It's a brilliant testament to the power of a church-based goods approach to social need, and it complements the state's provision perfectly, building on the infrastructure of Job Centres but bringing something unique and valuable to the table.

Complementary projects are perhaps the dream scenario for churches seeking a goods approach to social action. They make use of the state's provision while retaining their own unique and distinctive character, meaning that everybody wins. The only danger with this model is that churches might try to force themselves into it where the context doesn't invite it, most commonly because state provision is lacking or broken and therefore requiring contradiction or contrast.

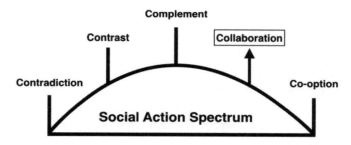

Next comes collaboration. Collaboration retains many of the features of the complementary model, but goes one step further in terms of the integration of the resources of church and state. Here congregations stand with the welfare state, designing, developing and delivering welfare services together. This mode of social action has grown significantly over the last two decades as government has increasingly turned to external organizations to deliver welfare services. As a result, congregations have formed partnerships to deliver education projects, family services, welfare support, social care and others besides. In some settings the local congregation acts as the principal provider and contract-holder, while in others it participates as a partner, stakeholder or even subcontractor. Either way, a church looking to collaborate with government can often find itself on the inside of discussions about the future of welfare provision.

Lifeline was started by congregations in Barking and Dagenham, Essex. Over the years the charity has delivered an impressive array of community projects in the borough. Riding the waves of contracts and cuts, the organization has become a key partner with the local authority and has gone on to develop Faith Action, a national initiative that works with government and local communities, equipping faith-based organizations to deliver services. With a previous government prioritizing early interventions, Lifeline won a number of contracts to develop children's centres for vulnerable young families. One of these was the Castle Point Children's Centre. An example of collaboration in action, Lifeline partnered with the local authority to build relationships with, and tailor services to, the needs of families in the area. Government funding enabled Lifeline to hire trained staff and offer nursery services, parenting training, language classes for mothers for whom English was a second language, and other services besides.

As this example shows, collaboration can have the particular benefit of drawing the resources of the state into the orbit of church social action, offering a level of scale and impact that would otherwise be unimaginable. The danger is that these resources may have attached to them the deficit-focused DNA of the state, leading to churches being forced to reshape their activities away from ones that promote relationship, creativity and joy and into the straitjacket of stifling bureaucracy and relentless targets. As we've seen, opportunities for collaboration are on the increase, as the government looks to outsource more and more activity. Churches therefore need to be mature and clear-sighted about exactly what respective collaborations will involve and preclude, and to judge their responses accordingly.

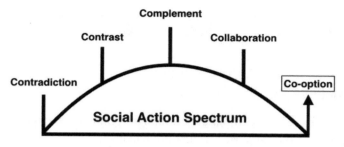

On the other end of the spectrum lies co-option. Here a congregation stands in for the state. In this mode the church is co-opted either explicitly or implicitly to carry out duties which are the proper responsibility of the state.

Many would argue that food banks represent an example of co-option, with churches picking up the pieces created by the state's failure properly to address the material deficits of a large and growing number of people.

It might be assumed that a goods approach would preclude churches from ever entering into such a co-option model. Certainly there are dangers with this model – namely that churches will end up permanently carrying out deficit-related activities that are properly the responsibility of the state. However, as food banks demonstrate, it may be entirely justifiable in some circumstances for churches to step into the gap of state failure if the only alternative is extreme deprivation and suffering on the part of the poorest and most marginalized. The critical factor is that churches should aim to do this as a temporary rather than permanent activity. Many churches running food banks have shown exactly this mindset, using them as a platform to campaign for changes in the welfare system and for more asset-based work which can tackle the root causes of food bank use (as the story of Life Church in the previous chapter vividly illustrates). If churches are to pursue a vision of social action which prioritizes the cultivating of assets

75

then they should be extremely wary of co-option, seeing it as a temporary measure to be employed only in extreme circumstances.

Standing up in different ways

As we have said throughout, no single point on the spectrum represents the definitive goods model of church social action. While the two extremes might present the most obvious challenges to a goods vision, each of the five modes or approaches can be the basis of meaningful social action and subsequently guide a congregation's interactions with the state.

Our findings also demonstrate that congregations seldom adopt a singular approach to social action. Given the increase in the scale and scope of these initiatives, and the varying issues that different communities and congregations are addressing, this is hardly surprising. Many congregations find themselves working on multiple fronts, deploying different strategies as they go. In particular, congregations that are socially active can quite naturally adopt all kinds of causes and campaigns. Leaders, members and volunteers bring their own individual callings, commitments and characters to bear on their sphere of engagement. As a result, many congregations find themselves operating simultaneously at different points of the spectrum. Take the congregations we belong to as the authors of this report: in any given week our churches deliver different types of social action to different groups. These activities include contradicting the state by campaigning on the treatment of refugees, providing contrasting services that offer care to homeless people, complementing the work of the local police in combating human trafficking, collaborating with the state to provide education for young people who have been excluded from school, and being co-opted by the health service to increase the number of people giving blood. The sign of a healthy church may not only be its number of social action projects but also its flexibility in adopting the most appropriate approach to a given issue in a particular climate and context.

For those churches starting from a smaller base in terms of resources or history of social action, the recent emergence of 'franchised' models of church social action can be of enormous benefit. These 'off-the-shelf' projects can make the first steps of engaging in local communities significantly easier for churches, freeing them from the need to 'reinvent the wheel' in terms of project design and governance. Of course there is a danger that such ease of implementation could side-track churches from the necessary consideration of the particularities of their own context and how their social action can cultivate assets rather than just address deficits, but with this caveat in mind the development of church social action franchises is to be warmly welcomed.[1]

Standing up and moving on

The churches that we have studied seldom adopt a singular approach to social action. Likewise, most resist a fixed stance. In many cases, the need to change or adapt our mode of social action is a sign of success. As we mentioned earlier, if a congregation runs a successful campaign and secures social change, then it is likely time to stop protesting and start working in other ways.

Churches' responses to the refugee crisis provide an excellent example of this. In September 2015, following a summer filled with tragic news stories about refugees, a group of church leaders gathered in Parliament. The gathering question was simple: how might local congregations helpfully respond to the crisis?

---

[1] See www.cinnamonnetwork.co.uk for further information on franchised church social action projects.

The first instinct was contradiction. Many joined campaigns by organizations such as Citizens UK that called on the UK government to do its bit on the nation's behalf in welcoming those displaced by the tragic situation in Syria. Under sustained pressure, the government eventually relented and set itself the target of welcoming 20,000 Syrian refugees by 2020. At this point some carried on down the path of contradiction, complaining that this was a paltry commitment and fighting to increase it.

Others, however, turned their minds to collaboration and the possibility of a refugee sponsorship scheme. This would make it possible for congregations to welcome and resettle refugee families here in the UK. There was a proven precedent for this approach in Canada. Since 1979, faith-based organizations, civil society and private citizens in Canada have welcomed more than 288,000 refugees on a similar programme. On the one hand, the attraction of the initiative is easy to see: here is a very practical way that congregations across the land could change the life of a family for ever and help their communities to become more welcoming. On the other hand, establishing such a scheme would be hugely complicated and could not be achieved without state support.

Collaboration wasn't easy at first, as the government was sceptical about the seriousness of civil society to do its part and thus about the feasibility of such a programme. As a result, groups like Church Response for Refugees collected names on a national register of those who would be prepared to welcome a family. For instance, Home for Good, a Christian adoption and fostering charity, had offers from more than 9,000 people willing to provide a home for an unaccompanied minor. Church leaders lobbied ministers and officials. Philanthropists stepped forward to fund those charities working on possible proposals. Within a matter of weeks the then Home Secretary, Theresa May, in her speech to the Conservative Party Conference, announced that she had instructed officials to explore the possibilities of a Canadian-style sponsorship scheme. The campaign had worked.

At this point churches and congregations had to change their approach. The leaders who had lobbied for the sponsorship scheme now found themselves on the inside. Suddenly Home Office officials and ministers were asking for their thoughts as to how this dream might come true. Before long, interested parties were meeting to develop a pilot scheme to establish the programme and prove the concept. To use the language often used by the officials themselves, the Community Sponsorship Scheme was 'co-constructed' by government, faith-based organizations and civil society. Ten months later a new Home Secretary, Amber Rudd, along with the Archbishop of Canterbury, Justin Welby, welcomed the first sponsored family of Syrian refugees to London. We should note that collaborating with government on one policy does not prevent churches from campaigning on related issues. Despite their success in campaigning for, and now collaborating with, government in the creation of community sponsorship, churches continue to campaign on a range of issues affecting refugees and asylum seekers, such as the plight of unaccompanied minors in Europe or the suffering of destitute asylum seekers currently residing in the UK without recourse to public funds.

In the Community Sponsorship Scheme we see the power of congregations first to impact government policy, and second to utilize different modes of social action as situations change. However, in other situations, partnership with government may decrease over time. Earlier we cited Lifeline, a charity collaborating with its local authority to deliver children's centres for disadvantaged families. Following the financial crisis in 2008, the council in the London borough of Barking and Dagenham was forced to make sweeping cuts. In 2010 the funding for the Castle Point Children's Centre was withdrawn, and the Lifeline team faced the possibility of closure. The charity was determined to honour the relationships that had been built, and sought to find a way to continue with the centre. The fear felt by families at the prospect of closure and the need for volunteers to take over from previously paid staff meant that the community took far greater ownership of the centre. Local parents, who had once been service users, became organizers, leaders and facilitators. With no budget for building maintenance and cleaners, community members took turns in the upkeep of the centre. While no longer collaborating so directly with the local authority, the Castle Point Children's Centre is now complementing reduced state provision, maintaining services that government can no longer afford and providing an even wider range of activities for local families. As change happens within communities, many congregations find new approaches to social action, adjusting the nature of their relationship with the welfare state as they go.

Standing up to change

Churches, like most associations, are notoriously conservative, even when their ethics and/or theology are progressive. What we have discovered is that the familiar perception is by no means always accurate. As we have seen from the start of this chapter, many churches have changed. Only a few decades ago, local churches delivered a minimal level of social action. Now it is a core and growing experience for congregations around the UK. As successive challenges and opportunities have come along, more and more congregations have taken a stand. Through contracts or cuts, the call to meet dire need or the courage to create new initiatives, churches have stepped up and stepped in time and again. Not everything is perfect and no single model provides the perfect blueprint for a goods approach to church social action. But if churches can be clearer on which model they are working with and what the likely opportunities and risks of such an approach will be, the future for church social action looks bright, both in terms of its impact on communities and in the renewal of the life of the church itself.

6

Recommendations for Church Social Action

The seventy-fifth anniversary of the Beveridge Report provides an opportunity to articulate a new vision for church social action and the potential for a new relationship between church and state as they relate to welfare and poverty. That vision has implications for a variety of different players across church and government.

The ten recommendations outlined below are intended to foster a vision of a society in which deficits are alleviated *and* goods are cultivated. The first five represent a challenge to the churches to develop a new vision for social action, focused on promoting goods rather than eliminating deficits. The second five are challenges for government, civil society and the churches in achieving a new settlement that recognizes and exploits the relative strengths of those involved in responding to issues of welfare and poverty in the UK.

A new vision for church social action

1 Denominations should reflect upon how they train and resource church leaders to develop and facilitate social action projects in general and in particular those that promote goods rather than simply address deficits.

2 Church leaders should regard social action as an essential element of discipleship and mission, deploying the resources at their disposal – such as time, money, people and buildings – in line with these commitments.

3 Church leadership teams should express their mission plans in the context of the goods that they wish to cultivate, and should evaluate the impact of their social action through that lens. They should communicate those plans in ways that their community can understand and embrace.

4 Congregations should be open to working with a wide range of partners in the community that share a similar vision of the goods.

5 The churches, especially on a national level, should continue to challenge government to maintain and strengthen the safety net provided by the welfare state so that deficits in society are properly and fairly addressed.

A new settlement between church and state

1 Government and civil society should establish a commission to examine, renegotiate and articulate a new relationship between statutory, corporate, voluntary and faith-based agencies and associations in their respective provision of public services relating to welfare and poverty.

2 Government and the churches should recognize and seek to coordinate their relative strengths of deficit reduction and goods promotion.

3 Government should prioritize involving churches and other faith organizations in community-building initiatives, and other initiatives that promote goods, above relying on them to deliver deficit reduction projects.

4 Government and the churches should identify areas for explicit partnership, in which statutory deficit-reduction work can be supplemented by, enhanced through or delivered within the vision of church-led goods-oriented social action.

5 Government and the churches should identify, evaluate and invest in innovative and high-quality examples of goods-oriented social action.

7

Evaluating Church Social Action

The following pages offer a series of community asset indicators, developed by Oasis, which churches can use to assess the level of development within their communities.[1] The indicators represent, for each of the goods identified in Chapter 1, general indications of the level of development of a community, based on Oasis's community hubs experience.

Community development is an imprecise process; it will always occur in different ways in different communities. There is a degree of overlap between the goods – they are interconnected and mutually supporting. For instance, a developed sense of relationship in a community will provide greater opportunities for partnership; a heightened sense of compassion will naturally lead individuals and the community as a whole to be more creative in developing responses to local need.

We hope that the indicators will provide a good sense of what churches should be looking for in fostering and delivering goods-oriented social action.

---

1 More information and resources available at www.openchurch.network.

Community asset indicators

Table 1: Relationship

Stage of community development			
Emerging	*Developing*	*Embedded*	*Transformative*
Some local community networks exist at a local (street) or functional (church, work, school) level. Occasional opportunities exist for local people to gather and to build relationships.	Community leaders (e.g. church leader, youth worker) intentionally build their own relationships into the community. Community development projects and events are formed through which individuals can develop relationships that exist beyond the local (street) or functional (e.g. church, work, school).	Members of the community intentionally seek out and build relationships with other community members. Community development projects and events attract and involve a diversity of people (across ages, genders, ethnicities, abilities) who are closely involved in designing and developing the project or event. Community development projects and events have the scale to provide structured volunteer opportunities.	Members of the community are empowered and enabled to develop new community-building initiatives and networks. Community development projects and events have the scale to provide both volunteer and paid opportunities to local people. Community relationships are characterized by interpersonal trust, enjoyment, support and understanding. Mutually supportive relationships are forged between different communities.

Table 2: Creativity

Stage of community development			
Emerging	*Developing*	*Embedded*	*Transformative*
Some local opportunities exist for people to express themselves (e.g. local sports club, choir).	Community develops and delivers opportunities for local people to express themselves and develop their sense of creativity (e.g. through sport, music or art). Appropriate venues are available for sport, music and artistic endeavour. Community provides signposting and encouragement towards appropriate vocational training opportunities.	Local people are empowered and enabled to develop new ways to express themselves. New cultural and artistic expressions emerge within community (e.g., artists' and craft groups, community arts projects, music festivals). Local people are empowered and enabled to develop their own solutions to the situations they encounter. Local people are empowered and enabled to harness their gifts to develop social enterprise. Community provides appropriate local vocational training opportunities.	Local people are fully supported to express themselves creatively, are fully alive and able to reach their God-given potential in life. The community is the home to a wide variety of embedded cultural and artistic expressions. Local people proactively share their knowledge and skills with each other. Local creativity is harnessed for the good of the community, with local people identifying, designing and delivering projects that respond to local need. The community is characterized by opportunity, imagination, improvisation, enterprise and creative endeavour.

Table 3: Partnership

Stage of community development			
Emerging	*Developing*	*Embedded*	*Transformative*
Leadership teams exist within community organizations.

Local collaborations beginning to emerge between community organizations. | Community leaders build empowered teams to develop community development projects and events and to respond to specific areas of need.

Local collaborations between organizations emerge into established partnerships, based on trust, respect and common priorities and objectives. | Members of the community naturally collaborate in teams to respond to community need.

Community organizations understand and appreciate their relative contribution to and potential for the community.

Community organizations develop, and work together towards, a neighbourhood plan. | Local people proactively engage in community organizing, in leading local organizations and in local politics.

Partnership working between organizations is successfully embedded. Joint funding applications are the norm.

Community proactively seeks out opportunities to support other communities, locally, nationally and internationally.

Community relationships are characterized by collaboration, partnership, negotiation, compromise, team work, collegiality and common endeavour. |

Table 4: Compassion

Stage of community development			
Emerging	*Developing*	*Embedded*	*Transformative*
Community support is typically focused on friends and family, with more occasional support for neighbours. There are a small number of organized opportunities for people to serve one another within the community (e.g. through church or other community organizations). The church community donates small amounts of time, resources and money.	Community members provide support to one another more proactively and intentionally. The church community has begun to identify needs and assets within the wider community and is taking steps towards addressing needs and building relationships. The church community donates time, resources and money to support the emerging response to community need.	Community members are actively engaged in caring for others in their local neighbourhood, both within the church and the wider community. The church community has a clear picture of the assets and needs of the wider community and has a proactive strategy for addressing need. People of all ages are involved in community service. The church community proactively and regularly donates time, resources and money in response to the strategy.	Community members are proactively engaged in caring for others in their local neighbourhood, their country and the world. There is a wide and varied range of organized opportunities for people to serve each another. Individuals and groups take initiative to develop their own approaches of caring for their neighbours. All community members joyfully donate significant amounts of their time, resources and money. Giving is an important and embedded commitment within the life of the community. Community relationships are characterized by generosity and humility, and therefore compassion.

Table 5: Joy

Stage of community development			
Emerging	*Developing*	*Embedded*	*Transformative*
Members of the church community feel they 'belong' within their congregation. There is pastoral support for those within the church community. A small number of events exist for community members to come together socially.	The church community is beginning to foster a sense of belonging both within the church congregation and the wider community. The church community provides a range of social activities for the entire neighbourhood at important moments in the year. Significant life stages and achievements are celebrated within the life of the church community.	The distinction between the church and wider community is blurred and the community is open and attractive to all. Community members feel a sense of belonging within their neighbourhood. All members of the community feel able to share and celebrate significant moments and achievements. There is a wide variety of regular opportunities for the entire neighbourhood to take part in social activities together, including large celebrations at key moments in the year. Activities cater for all ages and interests.	Community members share in the lives of one another and have developed a complex web of mutually supportive and inclusive relationships. The community demonstrates a spirit of celebration and all members of the community, including those on the fringes, are celebrated. The community provides excellent pastoral care for people at all stages of life. A spirit of abundance and joy pervades the neighbourhood and is an attractive force inviting others into relationship. Community members feel a sense of pride about their neighbourhood and actively encourage others to get involved.